How to make Greek and Natural Yogurt

The best homemade yogurt Recipes including

Frozen, Greek, Plain,
Vanilla, Coconut, Parfait, Smoothies,
Dips, ice cream.

Disclaimer

Published by Planet Gyrus Publication, Sunderland UK
Publisher Contact: publishing@planetgyrus.com

ISBN 978-0-9926334-3-1

Acknowledgments

I cannot make better use of this space other than to thank Lindsey, my wife. Although she calls me a "cooking fanatic", she has been the most patient when I am pursuing my culinary interests. In fact, she is the one who restores the kitchen to its original state once I am through.

I also dedicate this book to my late father-in-law Shaun McMahon. He would have been the happiest with the publication of this book. He's missed by the whole family. RIP!

I also want to dedicate this book to his sons, Thomas Anthony & Christopher Shaun, may their souls rest in peace. Even in their absence they give us the strength to continue.

Ian Owers

Contents

Acknowledgments 3

Introduction 12

Plain Yogurt 14

Why Make Your Own Yogurt? 15

It's Easy 15

It Costs Less 16

It's Safer 16

It's Tastier 17

It's Storable 17

It's Versatile 17

Health Benefits of Plain Yogurt 18

Prevents Gastrointestinal Disorders 18

Prevents and Treats Osteoporosis 19

Reduces Risk of Hypertension 19

Helps You Eat Less 20

Easier to Digest 20

Reduces Blood Cholesterol 21

Keeps Your Skin Healthy 21

Supplies & Equipment 22

Ingredients 22

Recipe 23

Troubleshooting 25

How to 'Thicken' the Yogurt 26

The Incubation Techniques 27

    In the Oven 28

    On a Heating Pad 28

    In the Microwave 28

    In a Cooler 29

Turning Plain Yogurt into Flavoured Yogurt 29

Frozen Yogurt 32

    Health Benefits of Frozen Yogurt 33

    When to Freeze 34

    Making Frozen Yogurt 34

        Still Freezing 34

        The Ice Cream Maker Method 35

Making Yogurt in a Crock Pot 37

    The Benefits 38

    Ingredients 38

    The Recipe 39

    Beware of the Taste 41

Greek Yogurt 43

    What is Greek Yogurt? 45

    Benefits of Greek Yogurt 45

        Variety of Uses 45

        Substitute for 'Fatty' Foods 45

Reduce Fat in Baked Goods..46

Get a Protein Boost 46

Feel Fuller, Longer...46

A Host of Other Vital Nutrients 47

Easier to Digest..47

Improves Digestion 47

Low on Sodium 48

Ingredients 48

Supplies & Equipment 49

Recipe 49

Yogurt Parfait 53

Benefits of Eating Yogurt Parfait 54

Healthy & Tasty 54

Nutritional Benefits 54

Variety of Ingredients 55

Flexibility..55

Boost Nutrition..55

A Full Meal 55

Ingredients 56

Tips & Tricks...56

Recipe 57

Things to Remember 58

Vanilla Yogurt 60

Health Benefits of Vanilla Yogurt.....................................60

Relieves Anxiety and Tension.................................60

Fight Claustrophobia.................................61

Fights Free Radicals & Toxins.................................61

Prevents Cancer 61

Aids Weight Loss.................................62

Supplies & Equipment 62

Ingredients.................................63

Recipe 64

Coconut Yogurt.................................68

Benefits of Coconut Yogurt 68

Source of Healthy Calories 68

Dairy for Vegans 69

Perfect for the Lactose Intolerant.................................69

Get a Vitamin Boost.................................69

An Additional Energy Boost.................................70

Helps Build Muscle 70

Preserves Your Teeth.................................70

Improves Metabolism 70

Healthier Hair and Skin.................................71

Reduces Inflammation 71

Ingredients & Supplies.................................71

Recipes.................................72

Yogurt Dip 76

Benefits 77

Customizable Ingredients...77

Sweet or Savoury 78

Takes No Time! 78

Easy As Pie!...78

Tastes Better...78

Costs Less 79

Absolute Control...79

Supplies & Equipment 79

Ingredients 80

Recipe 81

Yogurt Juice 83

Benefits of Yogurt Juice..83

Supplies & Equipment 83

Ingredients 84

Recipe 84

Yogurt Shake 86

Supplies & Equipment 87

Ingredients 87

Recipe 88

Yogurt Cocktail 89

Why Yogurt Cocktail?..90

Supplies & Equipment 90

Ingredients 91

Recipe 91

Yogurt Smoothie 93

   Benefits 94

      Smoothies Are Tasty.. 94

      Smoothies Are Fruity 94

      Smoothies Are Customizable 95

      Smoothies Are Filling 96

      Smoothies Contain Fibre................................. 97

   Fruit Choices.. 98

      • Citrus.. 98

      • Berries 98

      • Drupes.. 99

      • Melons.. 99

      • Tropical 99

      • Pomes 100

   Smoothie Tips: Putting the 'Smooth' in Smoothie 101

      Ice Cubes = Thickness................................... 101

      Use Frozen Fruit.. 101

      Liquids First.. 101

      Accelerate As You Go.................................... 102

   Ingredients 103

   Supplies & Equipment 103

   Recipes... 104

      Berry Smoothie... 104

      Tropical Smoothie... 105

Autumn Smoothie.. 106

Tropical Berry Smoothie 107

An Important Tip... 109

Yogurt Cake 111

What is Yogurt Cake?... 112

Why Eat Yogurt Cakes? 112

General Baking Tips Using Yogurt 113

When Using Butter 113

When Using Oils 113

When Using Sour Cream 113

When Using Water and Milk 114

Supplies & Equipment 114

Ingredients 114

Recipe 115

Yogurt Ice Cream 117

Benefits of Yogurt Ice Cream 118

Low Glycemic Index...................................... 118

Full of Calcium 118

Loaded with Proteins 119

It's Not Fattening 119

The 'Cold' Myth 119

Supplies & Equipment 120

Ingredients 121

Recipe 122

Part 1: 122

Part 2: 124

The Flavour 124

Yogurt Salad 126

Health Benefits of Eating Salads 126

Smoked Salmon Salad 127

Yogurt Salad Dressing for Chicken & Tangerine 127

Yogurt-Based Herb Salad Dressing 128

Yogurt Tahini Salad Dressing for Meatballs 128

Yogurt Salad Dressing and Roasted Cauliflower 128

Organic Plain Yogurt Dressing 129

Plain Yogurt Dressing to go with Arugula 129

Asparagus with Yogurt 129

Yogurt Dressing with Coleslaw 130

Persian Yogurt Salad 130

Yogurt Sundae 132

The Sundae vs. Parfait Debate 132

Supplies & Equipment 133

Ingredients 133

Recipe 135

Conclusion 138

Introduction

People have been making their own yogurt for over 4,000 years. It has been part of the staple diet across continents for many centuries. The health benefits of pure yogurt are well known and it is one of the most widely-consumed dairy products today.

Over the years, the commercial variants of yogurt have become popular and people prefer purchasing them instead of making yogurt at home. While purchasing it from the store is a convenient option, it prevents you from receiving many health benefits yogurt provides. Live and active cultures in natural yogurt are responsible for its health benefits and processed yogurt doesn't have that.

Yogurt is great for dealing with lactose intolerance, curing gastro-intestinal problems and enhancing milk protein digestion. Also, half a cup of yogurt is all you need to get half of your recommended daily intake of calcium. This is perhaps the easiest way to boost your nutrition.

The best way to enjoy yogurt while reaping its healthy properties is to make it at home. There are virtually endless recipes you can try. This is the purpose behind writing this book. I want to share my experiences in making different types of yogurts at home that I have learned over the years.

And who says making yogurt has to be boring? The recipes you will find in this book are simple to follow and a whole lot of fun to make.

From the hot desert of the Sahara to the cold winter of the Antarctic, yogurt can be consumed just about anywhere and provide its natural goodness. With several health benefits described in this book, you'll see no reason to give homemade yogurt making a try.

So, just read on till the end and enjoy the natural goodness of pure homemade yogurt, along with other healthy dairy products.

Plain Yogurt

Amid all the hullaballoo over the different types of yogurt, the flavoured, the fruity, the Greek and the liquefied, it is easy to forget that at its core, yogurt is a plain white dairy product. In this book, I have attempted to provide you as many yogurt-related recipes as I can, but they are incomplete unless you know how to make plain yogurt.

Image Link
:http://www.flickr.com/photos/citymama/3859846292/

Plain yogurt can be eaten on its own. It is the purest form of yogurt and is often referred to as regular yogurt. It is also the base for most of the recipes you will come across in this book. After all, you cannot make flavoured yogurt until you have made yogurt first.

This is why it is imperative that you learn how to make plain yogurt at home before moving on to any other recipes. As you will read later on, most recipes use yogurt as the key ingredient.

Why Make Your Own Yogurt?

Buying yogurt isn't the most arduous task in the world. You only need to walk down to the nearest market and you will find a shop which sells you natural and fresh yogurt. Yet, I would still recommend that you put in the effort and make your own.

The clichéd argument is that making your own dairy products ensures better quality and helps you monitor the ingredients. There is a reason I am suggesting making yogurt at home but at the same time will advise against churning your own butter: making yogurt is easy.

It's Easy

Think what you may about the process of making yogurt but one thing you cannot ignore is that it is quite easy to follow the recipe and complete the steps one by one. The effort required is minimal and the time it takes for you to get the yogurt ready is virtually unbelievable.

If it wasn't easy to make, I would have been the first guy to tell you that.

All you have to do is get the ingredients and supplies in order. I will detail the entire process step by step to make it easier for you to follow.

It Costs Less

There is a stark difference between the cost of making yogurt at home and buying it from a store. Yogurt brands have grown in popularity over the years. This has led to an increase in the price of all types of yogurt, including plain yogurt.

As a result, buying readymade plain yogurt has become a tad bit expensive for the average person. The ingredients required to make plain yogurt are minimal and most of them are available in your home. You can save a few pounds per litre of yogurt you make at home.

If you are an avid yogurt eater, making it at home could result in you saving hundreds of pounds every year.

It's Safer

You can contend that the plain yogurt being sold in the stores is safe to eat, being natural and fat-free. However, you cannot be absolutely certain about the ingredients if you actually see the product being made. There have been too many controversies regarding ingredients of food products and it is better to stay on the safe side than go for the riskier option.

When making plain yogurt at home, you are in complete control of the process. You can select the ingredients yourself, double checking them to ensure they are fit to use in the recipe. This way, you don't risk using any ingredients which may cause allergies or other side effects.

It's Tastier

Believe it or not, you can make better-tasting homemade plain yogurt than the version being produced commercially. There are numerous techniques you can use, not only to influence the taste of the yogurt you make but also its thickness and density. This way, you can have the taste and texture exactly match your preferences.

Most people eat yogurt regularly because of the health benefit it provides. However, being healthy doesn't mean it cannot be tasty. In fact, it will give you a whole new incentive to eat yogurt on a daily basis. If you are looking to improve your health and wellbeing, do so while enjoying the tangy taste of plain yogurt.

It's Storable

Homemade plain yogurt can be stored for up to two weeks without you having to worry about it getting spoiled. The only thing you have to consider for storing plain yogurt is using containers that have tight lids that seal shut properly. Then, simply put the containers in the fridge, retrieving them only when you want to eat the yogurt.

This gives you the luxury to make two weeks' worth of plain yogurt at once and then continue eating it as the days go by. Refill your containers by using the recipe to make more yogurt, around the 12th day or so.

It's Versatile

The best thing about plain yogurt is that it is versatile. You have the luxury of customizing the flavour according to your preference. This makes it easier for you to eat it, especially if you don't like the taste of regular yogurt much.

Also, plain yogurt is the base for many more recipes, including parfaits, smoothies, Greek yogurt, shakes, juices, etc. You can consume yogurt in any which way you want and benefit from the nutrition it delivers.

If you are not up for eating plain yogurt, you can follow any of the recipes provided later in the book and turn raw, plain yogurt into a tasty beverage or delicacy. This also makes it easier for you to convince your family to eat yogurt. They too will benefit from the nutrition it provides.

The ingredients and supplies required to make plain yogurt at home are easily available and in all likelihood, you will find them in your house. Plus, the recipe itself is quite straightforward. You don't have to be some sort of cooking expert to follow the recipe. Just go over the steps, one by one, and you will be able to make your own yogurt!

Health Benefits of Plain Yogurt

The health benefits of yogurt are numerous. One could write an entire book on the different ways yogurt is nutritious and enriching for the body. Small wonder 'eat yogurt' has become a catchphrase for health enthusiasts. If someone is looking to maintain their health and wellbeing and stay fit, yogurt is one of the best food items for them to eat.

Prevents Gastrointestinal Disorders

The presence of active cultures in plain yogurt makes it incredibly beneficial for your gut. With regular consumption, the microflora of the gut changes up. Plus the active cultures help food pass through the bowel quicker and they enhance the immune system.

What this does is make your digestive system better. Your body is able to ward off gastrointestinal disorders such as H. Pylori infection, diarrhoea, constipation and lactose intolerance. Can you believe the fact that eating yogurt can actually ensure you are able to eat other dairy products by preventing lactose intolerance?

Moreover, the risk of colon cancer is lower when the food is passing through your system much quicker than before. The nutrients responsible for these health benefits are the probiotics which you can get only from plain yogurt that has active cultures in it.

Prevents and Treats Osteoporosis

Osteoporosis is a disease in which the bone mass and density of a person gradually decrease. As a result, the bone structure gets weaker and there is a strong chance of fractures as well as other risks.

Yogurt contains two nutrients that are essential for bones, calcium and vitamin D, among others. Getting the daily recommended intake for both these vitamins makes your bones stronger and prevents osteoporosis.

People who are already suffering from the condition can alleviate it to a certain extent by adding yogurt to their diet. As their body gets the nutritional boost, the symptoms ease up and the disease becomes easier for them to manage.

Reduces Risk of Hypertension

Hypertension, or high blood pressure, is a common health issue faced by people today. There are a number of factors that can cause hypertension, including stress and an unhealthy diet. You can reduce the risk of hypertension by eating yogurt on a daily basis.

According to a study carried out on 5,000 participants, eating low-fat yogurt three times a day can reduce the risk of hypertension by 50%. Even people who are genetically predisposed to high blood pressure can prevent the condition from occurring.

Hypertension is a dangerous health problem which can lead to heart attack, stroke and other coronary issues. Reducing the risk for hypertension can have a profound impact on your overall health.

Helps You Eat Less

If you are trying to lose weight, one of the most effective techniques is to reduce your food intake. However, that isn't possible if you don't feel full after a meal. This is a common hurdle faced by many people when they are on the road to weight loss. They keep on eating simply because they don't feel full after the meal due to the smaller portions.

Plain yogurt contains a lot of protein. Protein can make you feel full even without actually having to eat that much. You can substitute your meals with yogurt and the different yogurt based recipes I will tell you about later on in the book.

You can reduce both your food and calorie intake, yet not experience the feeling of hunger or starvation. This is why you should make eating yogurt a habit as it can boost your weight loss efforts considerably.

Easier to Digest

Yogurt not only helps improve the functioning of your digestive system, it itself is easy to digest. What this means is that the nutrients present in yogurt are absorbed by your body quicker because it passes through swiftly. With other foods, the metabolism slows down nutrient absorption.

This is quite unlike milk, which can be difficult to digest, especially for people suffering from lactose intolerance. Plain yogurt with active cultures is a safe dairy product for people with mild lactose intolerance, purely because it is easy to digest.

You can replace milk with yogurt, but only if it contains cultures. Bacteria breaks down lactose which helps yogurt go through the digestive tract easily.

Reduces Blood Cholesterol

Along with preventing hypertension, eating yogurt keeps your cardiovascular system healthy by regulating the blood cholesterol level. Your body needs cholesterol, but not the bad kind. Adding yogurt to your daily diet can help control bad cholesterol.

Once again, the live cultures in yogurt work their magic. Moreover, eating plain yogurt can help bind bile acids.

Both these result in your blood cholesterol level decreasing considerably. If you are having trouble keeping it in check, it is time you start making plain yogurt at home and eating it regularly.

Keeps Your Skin Healthy

Plain yogurt works wonders for your skin. It ensures your skin remains healthy so that you look younger and more vibrant. Eating yogurt will also help your skin cells fight the signs of aging. This is far easier and more economical than using beauty products.

Apart from eating plain yogurt as it is, you can make a mask by combining it with olive oil and honey. Put the mixture on your face for half an hour and then rinse it off.

Your skin becomes more radiant and will glow as a result of this treatment.

Yogurt will boost your body's immune system, enabling it to fight common diseases and illnesses like the common cold, flu, etc. As you can see from the health benefits of plain yogurt, eating 2 to 3 servings a day is a good remedy to stay healthy.

Supplies & Equipment

To make plain yogurt at home, you will need to procure some equipment and supplies. I have added a chapter on the different methods of incubating yogurt. You can choose any of the methods and you will have to get the relevant equipment to properly incubate the yogurt mixture.

The recipe requires that you use a quart of milk, which has to be heated before you can put mix in the yogurt starter. So, you need a saucepan that is big enough to hold a quart of milk.

You will also require a mixing bowl in which the ingredients will be combined. The yogurt starter and milk have to be whisked together so you will require something to whisk the mixture with.

Also, set out a container large enough to accommodate the mixture that you form when the ingredients have been whisked together. The container can also be used to store the plain yogurt once it is ready to eat. Keep it in the fridge and it remains good for a couple of weeks at least.

Ingredients

To make plain yogurt, you require three main ingredients:

> ➢ 2 tbsp yogurt starter – the yogurt starter should have active bacteria. The bacteria not only provides the

health benefits but is responsible for the tangy taste of plain yogurt. Furthermore, it helps 'cook' the yogurt and bring it to its final form.

➤ ½ cup dry milk powder – dry milk powder is used to speed up the process of making plain yogurt. It is added to the milk you use for the recipe.

➤ 1 quart milk – there are no restrictions on the type of milk you use but I would recommend that you go for low-fat or 2% milk. This makes the yogurt non-fattening and you can eat it as much as you like without having to worry about putting on weight.

These three ingredients are pretty much all you need. Be consistent with your choice of milk as the plain yogurt base will be used for most of the other recipes described in this book.

It is a good idea to make plain yogurt a couple of times, using different kinds of milk each time. This way, you can check the impact each type of milk has on the flavour and texture of the yogurt and don't have to go by trial and error.

Recipe

To make things easier for you, the recipe for plain yogurt has been laid out in a step by step format. You shouldn't have much trouble following the instructions provided here. In fact, all the recipes in this book will follow the same format, so trying them out shouldn't be a problem.

➤ The first thing you need to do is heat the milk up. Pour the quart of milk into the saucepan and put it on the stove on high heat. You have to get the temperature up to at least 180°F so it will take you around 15 minutes to get there.

However, you don't have to boil the milk. Turn the stove off as soon as you see the bubbles forming at the top. It doesn't take long for the milk to spill over, so be careful. Also, don't leave the milk unsupervised as you cannot afford to burn it. Or else, it will be unusable for this recipe.

➤ When the milk starts heating up, add dry milk powder to it. Use a wooden spoon to stir the dry milk powder in. Make sure it mixes perfectly with the milk.

➤ After the milk has reached the desired temperature, move it from the hot stove. Place it in a cooler spot as you have to cool it. Keep it there for at least 30 minutes. You can use a cooler for this purpose. However, I wouldn't recommend putting it in the fridge.

➤ Take a pittance of the milk and pour it into the mixing bowl. A few tablespoons will do the trick. Add the yogurt to the milk and start whisking. The ingredients have to blend thoroughly with each other so whisk vigorously. At the same time, make sure the mixture doesn't spill on to the counter.

➤ Once the yogurt starter and milk are combined, pour the mixture into the container. Put the lid on the container and wrap it in a towel. Place it in a secluded corner where it won't be touched. It has to be kept there for over 8 hours so choose a spot wisely.

Putting the yogurt aside to let it stand for a few hours is known as the incubation period. This is when the live cultures get the chance to work their

24

magic. They start taking effect right away and lend all their nutritional goodness to the plain yogurt.

Don't open the lid of the container, even if only to steal a peek at the yogurt, before 8 hours. The longer you keep it, the firmer the yogurt will be. Moreover, the flavour is tangier if you let the yogurt stand for 12 hours.

➢ When you feel the yogurt is ready to eat, remove the towel from around the container and put it in the fridge. This helps halt the culturing process. The cultures have had more than enough time to do their thing. If they still haven't produced the desired result, it is quite likely the yogurt starter you used didn't have active cultures.

After a couple of hours, remove the container from the fridge and enjoy your plain yogurt!

Troubleshooting

When trying this recipe for the first time, there is every chance that it may not work the way you expected it to. If you stick to the recipe and follow the steps in the correct order, there shouldn't be any issue with the consistency, taste, or texture of the plain yogurt you make.

The problem most people trying this recipe for the first time face is that the yogurt doesn't turn out to be firm enough. The likely cause of this issue is that they didn't let it stand for long enough. It is quite tempting to check on it from time to time.

The other cause could be that you didn't let the milk cool down enough before mixing in the yogurt. Apart from that, there should be no reason for the yogurt to not become firm. Unless of course the yogurt you used didn't have active cultures, in which case there is nothing you can do but go back to the drawing board.

However, just because the yogurt hasn't firmed up doesn't mean that you should throw it out. It is perfectly usable and you can make smoothies or shakes with it. The recipes for both will be provided later on in the book.

How to 'Thicken' the Yogurt

You can avoid the dilemma of opening the container and finding out that the yogurt you made isn't firm enough. There are some thickening techniques you can use to ensure the yogurt achieves the desired firmness and thickness. Let's look at some that you can use:

- As mentioned above, letting the yogurt sit for longer makes it firmer. According to my own experience, the yogurt starts firming up around the 6-hour mark, which makes 8 hours more than sufficient to achieve the desired texture. Of course, you can let it stand for 12 hours or more.
- The second technique is to heat up the milk beyond the recommended temperature. Not only that but you should try to keep it on the heat for a few minutes before removing it from the stove. Once again, make sure the milk doesn't start boiling.
  What this does is allow the sogginess and moisture in the milk to evaporate. The solids contained in the milk start taking hold and they combine with the active cultures in the yogurt starter to make the plain yogurt firmer.
- Straining yogurt is a technique used for making Greek yogurt (recipe later in the book). After the yogurt is ready, you put it on cheese cloth or a mesh

strainer of any kind to let it drain. Leave it for 12 hours or so to let the yogurt becomes really thick. Straining will remove whey from the yogurt, which essentially turns plain yogurt into Greek yogurt.

- Use non-fat dry milk powder instead of any other type. It helps make the yogurt thicker. Add ½ cup of dry milk powder per quart of milk to get the recipe right. Using non-fat milk along with non-fat dry milk powder is the best way to go.
- There is one other way but it is not particularly healthy. Adding a tablespoon of gelatine to the mixture before whisking will not only make it thicker and firmer, but also creamier. Pectin is another ingredient you can add but I would suggest you use any of the four methods above instead of this one.

As you can see, there are several ways you can make plain yogurt firmer and thicker. Follow the right technique and you won't have to be disappointed when you finally open the container and check the thickness and firmness of the plain yogurt you made.

The Incubation Techniques

A yogurt maker is a solid investment, should you want to spare the cash for it. It helps speed things along and makes it easier for you to get the right taste and firmness for the plain yogurt you make. It will also help you make other recipes covered in this book.

However, there are equally effective ways to incubate your plain yogurt mixture without a yogurt maker. You can still buy one if you want to, but you don't need to.

Coming to the point, here are some incubation techniques you can follow to let the yogurt reach its correct firmness and thickness.

In the Oven

The first technique is putting the yogurt mixture in the oven. Heat up your oven to 100°F and then put the quart jar inside. Make sure the container is safe to use in the oven. You don't need to wrap the container. In fact, you don't even have to keep an eye on it.

The best approach to take is by putting it in the oven at night before going to bed. When you wake up and remove the container from the oven, you will be greeted by perfect, plain yogurt. Keep the oven door closed and it will maintain that temperature throughout the incubation process. Let it sit for 10 to 12 hours.

On a Heating Pad

This one is a practical technique, but only if you have a heating pad at home. If you don't, use any of the other methods described here. The method is quite simple. You simply have to wrap the container in towels and place it on the heating pad.

The heating pad maintains a consistent temperature at around 100°F. Here too you have to let the yogurt sit for a good 8 to 10 hours before you can open the lid and check its firmness.

In the Microwave

You can use your microwave to incubate the plain yogurt as well. Before you place the container in it, you have to make sure it is properly insulated. For this, you have to use a number of towels. Also, wrap the container in foil.

Run the microwave for 4 to 5 minutes. The towels will ensure the heat remains trapped inside for a few hours at least. It provides the right environment to incubate the yogurt.

In a Cooler

This one is also a simple technique. Boil water in a kettle. Use two kettles if you can. Once the water is boiled, put the kettles into the cooler. They will emit steam and create a warm environment inside the cooler. Leave it as it is for 10 to 15 minutes and then place the yogurt container in the cooler.

Wrap the container in a towel as the steam is bound to create heat and moisture inside the cooler. Leave the container in there for around 8 hours and you're good to go.

These are just some of the incubating methods you can use when making plain yogurt. Incubation is also a part of the process for some of the other recipes described later on in this book. So, it is a good idea to find a technique that works and keep using it throughout.

A word of warning here is appropriate. Even though I have found these incubation methods to work, there are no guarantees that the yogurt will achieve the firmness and thickness you are looking for. Hence, I would suggest you follow the tips provided above for making yogurt thicker in combination with these incubation techniques to achieve the best possible results.

Turning Plain Yogurt into Flavoured Yogurt

Once you have made plain yogurt, you can start experimenting with its taste. Yogurt, in its purest form, possesses a salty and tangy taste. Needless to say, it isn't as palatable as the fruity yogurt you can buy at the store. Well, no one is stopping you from making it tasty!

That's right. You can turn plain yogurt into flavoured yogurt quite easily. The technique for it is simple. Plus, there is an endless list of flavours to select from. Choose any fruit you want to add to the yogurt and make a fruity treat for yourself.

Or, if you are in the mood for something savoury, you can add spices and sauces to the yogurt. Any ingredients you add to plain yogurt will turn it into flavoured yogurt and it will become much easier for you to eat it.

In all likelihood, you will prefer to add fruits to the yogurt in order to sweeten its flavour. According to flavoured yogurt sales, the top ten flavours are:

1. Vanilla
2. Chocolate
3. Strawberry
4. Lemon
5. Orange
6. Blackberry
7. Peach
8. Blueberry
9. Raspberry
10. Mango

To make it easier for you to understand the process of turning plain yogurt into flavoured yogurt, I will take blackberry as the flavour of choice (the recipe for vanilla yogurt comes later in the book).

I am assuming that you have made plain yogurt by this stage and are ready to turn it into flavoured yogurt. The first thing you need to do is remove the stems from the blackberries, if they have stems that is. In fact, it is better if you buy blackberries that have no stems. This will make things easier.

Next, cut the blackberries into halves and toss them in the blender. Keep blending till the blackberries are thoroughly chopped up. Take ¼ cup of plain yogurt you have made and put it into a mixing bowl. Extract the crushed blackberries from the blender and add to the yogurt. Whip the yogurt till the blackberries are mixed into it. The yogurt should start taking on the colour of the blackberries.

Puree the blackberries and yogurt till they form a smooth and creamy mixture. Now, you can eat it up but if you feel the quantity is limited or the flavour of the blackberries is strong, pour some more yogurt into the blender and give it another go. That is it. Simply replace blackberries with any fruit of your choice and turn your plain yogurt into flavoured yogurt.

Like I said, there are no restrictions as far as the choice of flavour is concerned. The aim is to get you to eat yogurt!

So, now you know how to make plain yogurt at home. Though you can eat it as is, the main purpose of plain yogurt is to serve as a base for the other recipes you will find in this book. Read on till the end and you will see for yourself!

Frozen Yogurt

One of the most popular types of yogurt is frozen yogurt. As the name suggests, frozen yogurt is made with ingredients that are frozen beforehand. This is why it is known as a healthier alternative to ice cream.

Many companies today make frozen yogurt. In fact, a trip to the department store is all you need to restock your frozen yogurt. It's a $200 million industry and there is little to suggest the number won't go up in the future.

Image Link:
http://www.flickr.com/photos/galant/2552806737/

But why should you spend your hard-earned money on buying frozen yogurt when you can make your own healthier version at home? You might wonder if it is really worth the time and effort. Trust me, it is. Here are some great reasons why you should make frozen yogurt at home.

Health Benefits of Frozen Yogurt

- Frozen yogurt is a low-fat food. Commercially available ice cream has more than 15% fat but in frozen yogurt; the percentage comes down to 0.5. That is almost no fat at all!
- The low fat density of frozen yogurt also ensures its calorie count is low. People who are watching their weight can consume frozen yogurt if they absolutely must have a sweet treat.
- Frozen yogurt contains all the nutrients and elements contained in freshly made yogurt. From a rich dose of calcium to substantial quantities of zinc, potassium and selenium, the list of nutrients is long. What's more is that your body needs most of them on a daily basis.
- There is a wide variety of flavours you can choose from, giving you enough range to have frozen yogurt multiple times a day. According to nutrition experts, the average adult should consume three portions of dairy products every day. Frozen yogurt is a great option for covering all three servings.
- The recipe is easy and you only need to use a couple of ingredients. In other words, there is no reason for you not to make frozen yogurt at home.

When to Freeze

Frozen yogurt isn't really made by freezing yogurt after you have made it. Rather, you have to freeze the mixture or ingredients before making it.

The amount of time for which you need to freeze the mixture depends on the method you follow. There are two main methods which we will discuss in the next part of this chapter.

When you are making fruit-flavoured frozen yogurt, you will need frozen fruits. For instance, if you are making peach frozen yogurt, freeze the peaches before you start.

Making Frozen Yogurt

There are two main ways of making frozen yogurt. The one you choose depends mainly on whether or not you have an ice cream maker at home. An ice cream maker speeds up the freezing process so the frozen yogurt can be prepared quickly. On the other hand, it is a major investment and you might be apprehensive about the cost.

You don't need to worry, as you can still make tasty frozen yogurt without an ice cream maker. Listed below are the steps you have to follow.

Still Freezing

The process by which you make frozen yogurt without an ice cream maker is known as "still freezing". For this, you have to combine all the ingredients you are using (we will come to that later). Then, start beating them well. You have to make sure that the ingredients are mixed well.

They don't usually reach the desired level of thickness till you give the process its due time. At least after the second beat you can say that the mixture is in a consumable state.

Once this is done, just place the mixture in the freezer and you're good to go.

The only drawback to this method is the lack of consistency. The thickness and texture of the frozen yogurt depends hugely on how long it has been mixed.

When talking about beating the ingredients together, you can opt for one of two approaches:

- **Using a Mixer:** Combine all the ingredients in a bowl and wrap it up with foil. Place the bowl in the freezer for a couple of hours so that the mixture hardens. Then, use a mixer to beat the mixture a couple of times. Your frozen yogurt is ready.
- **Using a Food Processor:** You also have the choice of using a food processor to beat the mixture instead of a mixer. Whichever machine you have available will do the trick. Even the process remains the same. The only difference is that you have to break the frozen mixture before it can be put into the food processor.

Either way, you will end up with a bowl of wholesome, pure frozen yogurt you can consume right away. Garnish it with nuts or pieces of fruit, depending on your personal preference.

You can serve the yogurt as soon as you have finished beating it. Also, you can place it in the freezer to freeze it some more before serving.

The Ice Cream Maker Method

If you have an ice cream maker, you can use it to make yogurt as well. I'm sure this is something you would not have thought of when you were purchasing the ice cream maker. You may have made some great ice cream at home before, but you can now try your hand at frozen yogurt.

The first thing you need to check is whether you have to freeze the container in which you make ice cream. It varies from machine to machine. You might have to put it in the freezer for five to six hours to get it to the temperature needed to make frozen yogurt.

The great thing here is that you can make the yogurt mixture exactly the way you did for the still freezing method. Hence, you don't have to learn anything new if you have tried the method described before.

All you have to do is put the mixture into the frozen container to let it freeze. The machine will mix the yogurt and smoothen it for you to eat. Just wait for the mixture to freeze and then you can scoop it out of the machine. Also, turn off the machine once the mixture is frozen. You can add any nuts or fruits you want to have with the frozen yogurt.

Again, you have the option of putting the yogurt in the freezer to freeze it a little more.

Regardless of the method you use or the number of hours you freeze it for, it won't have much of an impact on the quality or texture of the frozen yogurt. You can also add the ingredients you want to the frozen yogurt.

So, when it is so easy to make frozen yogurt at home, why spend money on buying the processed, commercial version which doesn't even deliver the natural flavour and nutritional value of yogurt?

Making Yogurt in a Crock Pot

One of the best ways to preserve the cultures and keep them active throughout is to make yogurt in a crock pot. A crock pot, also known as a slow cooker, is a dish in which, well, you cook food slowly. The actual process of making yogurt is quick and you don't need to spend more than half an hour on it.

However, you will have to let the mixture sit for at least 12 hours. This is what the cultures need to stay alive and healthy. Only then will they remain active enough to provide you the health benefits of homemade yogurt you are looking for. The first tip for you here is to get the mixture ready and then go to sleep. When you wake up, the creamy yogurt will be ready to eat!

Image Link:
http://www.flickr.com/photos/misscrabette/4624585599/

But before you do that, you need to know how to make yogurt in a crock pot. Firstly, you need to have a crock pot. If you don't own one, it is a worthwhile investment.

The Benefits

While there aren't any specific benefits of making yogurt in a crock pot, it does allow you to enjoy the health benefits of yogurt. Processed yogurts don't have active bacteria (cultures) which is the source of most health benefits yogurt offers.

Then there are the inherent advantages of slow cooking. The yogurt's flavour is distributed more evenly and you get to enjoy the tangy taste of pure yogurt.

At the same time, it reduces the effort required to make yogurt at home. In fact, the most difficult thing to do is stay away from the yogurt while it is sitting in a crock pot. That's right; you just have to let the milk and yogurt stay as is for around 12 hours while you eat, sleep, rest, go to work, etc.

Ingredients

Now to the ingredients:
- ½ gallon milk
- ½ cup plain yogurt

That is it as far as the ingredients are concerned. You don't need anything else to make yogurt in a crock pot. You might be wondering how you can actually make yogurt if you are using plain yogurt in the recipe. This is the magic of it. You get to enjoy better active cultures by making yogurt in a crock pot. The yogurt you use is called the 'yogurt starter'.

This is why you have to check the yogurt ingredients you purchase to use in this recipe. The key is to go over the label on the back. You have to make sure there are ACTIVE CULTURES in the yogurt. Under no circumstances should you get yogurt that doesn't have active cultures in it. Otherwise, it is not fit to use in this recipe.

As far as milk is concerned, you can use raw milk but that will add to the time you need to let the mixture sit. So, it is better to go for whole milk. There are no restrictions as far as the brand is concerned. You just need to have ½ gallon of milk.

Also, you need a saucepan that is big enough for ½ gallon milk. In addition, you should keep two towels or cloths on hand to use once you start following the recipe.

The Recipe

To make yogurt in a crock pot, you simply have to follow the recipe listed below step by step.

> Set the crock pot on high. You have to heat the milk so start by turning the crock pot on.

> Put the yogurt in a bowl and place it on the counter while you get the crock pot ready. This will get the yogurt nice and warm when you get to the main part.

> Next, pour the milk into the saucepan and place it on the stove to get it to boil. This will take away the rawness and make it ready for the recipe. For this, the ideal temperature is 185°. Make sure you don't leave the milk unsupervised even for a minute. You cannot afford for it to boil over the saucepan or burn and get stuck to the bottom.

➤ When the milk is about to get ready, turn on the tap in the sink and fill it up with water. Put some ice in the water. You need to let it get cold as you have to place the hot saucepan in it.

➤ Once the milk starts bubbling, turn off the heat and place the lid on the saucepan. Then, grab the towels and transfer the saucepan to the sink. Keeping the lid on is important so that none of the water goes into the milk. The important thing to remember is that the milk shouldn't get cold. You need to cool it but not for more than 10 minutes. The recipe requires pouring warm milk into the crock pot.

➤ You have to turn the crock pot off when you remove the saucepan from the sink. By this point, the crock pot will be at the right temperature for you to start making yogurt.

➤ Now, pour 1 cup of milk along with yogurt starter into the crock pot. Start whisking till the two blend and mix well together. Be gentle as you don't want the mixture to spill over. Once you have whisked them together, pour the remaining milk into the container as well while stirring. Check again to ensure your crock pot is turned off. You cannot have the mixture heating up.

➤ Once this is done, wrap the crock pot in towels. It is better to use towels as they allow the moisture to remain inside the crock pot. You have to let it sit for 8 to 12 hours, depending on how creamy the yogurt is at that point. It is around the 8-hour mark that the yogurt's taste starts getting tangy. After that, every hour you let it rest, the tangier it will get.

> At no point are you to open up the towels and check the yogurt. When you are trying this recipe for the first time, don't peek before 8 hours. This is the minimum number of hours you have to wait for before you can check the yogurt's state. I know it is quite tempting to keep checking the yogurt but if you want to let it culture, you have to stay patient.

> Even when you open up the towels and check the yogurt, you cannot touch or taste it right away. If you wait for 8 hours, there is no doubt that you will find creamy yogurt waiting for you inside the crock pot. Don't stir, move, taste or shake the yogurt just yet. You have to get it to firm up a little. For this, you have to put the crock pot in the fridge as is. Allow it to cool for a couple of hours and it will be ready. You can even keep it in there longer if you are occupied with something else. The time for which you keep the yogurt in the fridge has no bearing on its taste or texture whatsoever.

> Take the crock pot out from the fridge and start transferring the yogurt to the container you want to keep it in. Mason jars are handy for this purpose but you can use any vessel you prefer.

> The yogurt is ready to eat. You can keep it in the fridge for storage and use it over a period of time.

Beware of the Taste

Often people are surprised at how tangy yogurt made in a crock pot is. The reason is that they are used to eating flavoured or processed plain yogurt. The cultures in that yogurt aren't active so the tanginess goes away. So, you have to beware of the taste of your homemade yogurt in a crock pot. It will be tangy.

You have the luxury of sweetening it up a little, provided you don't use sugar. That will take away much of the nutritional value and health benefits you receive through yogurt. You can add fresh fruits or raw honey to the yogurt. However, the best option is to eat it as is.

Regardless of how you choose to eat the yogurt made in a crock pot or the flavour you add to it, you will still get to enjoy the benefits of live cultures. Hence, it is a great recipe for you to try should you want to eat some healthy, pure yogurt.

And not to forget the fact that it doesn't cost much. If you have a crock pot at home, you only need to bear the cost of a container of yogurt and a carton of milk. That is all you need to make the purest yogurt which promises a host of health benefits at home!

So, now you have learned to make yogurt in a crock pot. Keeping all the recipes for making yogurt in mind, this might be the easiest. You only need to combine a couple of ingredients in a crock pot and let them sit for a few hours. Making yogurt at home couldn't get any easier!

Greek Yogurt

Greek yogurt is a superfood in its truest sense. A single serving of Greek yogurt is more nutritious than three ounces of lean meat. Though it has grown immensely popular over the years, the commercial variants of this superfood are not up to the mark.

The issue is, again, the lack of regulation. There is no way to check whether the yogurt you buy is healthy. So, some brands get away with slapping the 'Greek' label on any yogurt product they want.

Image Link:
http://www.flickr.com/photos/theimpulsivebuy/962216610
6/

So, it is important that you know what Greek yogurt exactly is. Since most people are unfamiliar with what Greek yogurt actually is and what sets it apart from other types of yogurt, they cannot tell the difference.

What is Greek Yogurt?

Greek yogurt is like regular yogurt but without the whey. Whey is the soggy part of milk that is left once it has been curdled. Due to the absence of whey, Greek yogurt is thicker and creamier than other types of yogurt. This lends it a nice texture and feel.

Moreover, removing whey from yogurt makes it more nutritious. It's not that plain yogurt is not nutritious and healthy, but without whey, there is less sugar and carbohydrates, and more protein. In other words, it is superior to other types of yogurt in terms of nutrition.

Benefits of Greek Yogurt

Compared to other types of yogurt, Greek yogurt is more expensive. It is more economical for you to make it at home than buy it from the store. But, is it worth the time and effort? Yes, it is. There are numerous benefits of Greek yogurt.

Variety of Uses

You can choose to make flavoured or plain Greek yogurt. Either way, its versatility enables you to put it to a variety of uses, particularly plain yogurt. For one, you can substitute plain Greek yogurt in any recipe you make when using regular yogurt. This will make the recipe healthier and more nutritious for you.

Substitute for 'Fatty' Foods

There are a lot of complementary food items that have high fat content. You can use Greek yogurt as a substitute for:
- Cream
- Ice cream
- Mayonnaise

- Sour cream

You can switch Greek yogurt for these items in any recipes you follow. It will make the recipe healthier and maybe even tastier! Greek yogurt has less fat than all of these.

Reduce Fat in Baked Goods

You can also reduce fat in baked goods by adding Greek yogurt to the recipe. For instance, if you are baking a cake, you can add some Greek yogurt to the frosting. For other recipes, simply replace the 'wet' ingredients in the recipes with Greek yogurt and the item will become less fatty.

Get a Protein Boost

As mentioned above, removing whey from yogurt increases the amount of protein it contains. In fact, a single serving of Greek yogurt contains around 23 grams of protein. That is almost 50% of protein the average adult needs to consume daily. Make sure the yogurt is fat-free to enjoy the protein boost. When compared to regular plain yogurt, the protein quotient is nearly double.

Feel Fuller, Longer

The added advantage of getting your daily protein intake is that you feel fuller for a longer period of time. Hence, eating Greek yogurt daily can reduce your overall food intake without compromising your health or making you feel hungry.

As you can see, most health benefits mentioned here will aid your weight loss efforts. If you are looking to shed the extra pounds, adding Greek yogurt to your daily diet is a great idea.

A Host of Other Vital Nutrients

Protein isn't the only vital nutrient you can get through Greek yogurt. There are a host of other nutrients your body needs on a daily basis. Among the most important ones are:

- Vitamins A, B & D12
- Calcium
- Potassium
- Phosphorus
- Niacin
- Riboflavin

The nutritional qualities are what make Greek yogurt much healthier than other types of yogurt. Eating it regularly ensures you don't suffer from any nutritional deficiencies and your health remains intact.

Easier to Digest

Greek yogurt is easier to digest than other types of yogurt. This is because of its lower lactose content than plain yogurt and flavoured yogurt. This also makes it safer to eat for people who suffer from mild lactose intolerance. If you face the same problem, Greek yogurt is one of the few dairy products you can eat without any issues.

Improves Digestion

In addition to being easy to digest, Greek yogurt also improves your digestion. It is a great source of probiotics that strengthen the digestive system and improve its functioning. Probiotic bacteria is great for keeping the digestive system clean. This will help prevent conditions such as diarrhoea as well as irritable bowel syndrome (IBS). This is the reason that probiotics are sold separately as dietary supplements and considered a superfood.

Low on Sodium

Consuming excessive sodium can lead to several health problems, primarily cardiovascular diseases. Hypertension and coronary disease are some of the likely outcomes. This is why most people today are looking to reduce the amount of sodium in their diet. Greek yogurt is the perfect food to add to your diet to avoid consuming too much sodium. Compared to regular yogurt, Greek yogurt contains 50% less sodium.

These are the numerous health benefits of making Greek yogurt at home and eating it. Keep in mind that there are many more. You will only realize that when you start making and eating Greek yogurt.

Plus, the great thing about it is that you don't need to put in any extra effort to make Greek yogurt. It is as easy as making plain yogurt so the recipe itself is quite simple to follow. All you need to do is make some space in your fridge and then just sit back and relax for a couple of hours.

Ingredients

The two main ingredients to make Greek yogurt are milk and yogurt with active cultures. This is pretty much the same base you used to make yogurt parfait. There are a few considerations you need to make when selecting the type of milk you use.

There are no restrictions on the type of milk you use. You can choose from regular milk, low-fat milk, whole milk and even skimmed milk. You can also use dry milk but you will have to culture it before you start following the recipe. The yogurt's texture and thickness will differ depending on the type of milk you use.

You might have to try the recipe a couple of times before you discover the best one. In fact, you can also use almond milk or soy milk. Once again, you will have to culture it to be effective enough to be used in the recipe.

As far as the yogurt is concerned, you can use freeze-dried yogurt starter. Or else, you also have the option of using plain yogurt that has live and active cultures.

You will need 8 cups of milk and 4 tablespoons of plain yogurt. This will allow you to make 6 cups of Greek yogurt. You can adjust the quantity of ingredients in order to increase the yield.

Supplies & Equipment

To make Greek yogurt, you require a few supplies along with the ingredients. First are the containers. As you will note throughout this book, most recipes to make yogurt at home utilize containers of some kind. So, make sure you have the right equipment before you start.

Coming back to Greek yogurt, you need one ½-pint-sized jar and two quart-sized jars. Each jar should have lids as they will come in useful later on. Along with jars, you also need a thermometer, a cooler, cheese cloth and a mesh strainer.

The milk has to be heated so get a pot big enough for 8 cups of milk. The pot should be a heavy-bottomed one.

Get the equipment and supplies ready before the ingredients. The entire recipe shouldn't take more than an hour but only if you have all the items you need at hand.

Recipe

Follow the steps below to make Greek yogurt perfectly. Sticking to the recipe ensures you get it right the first time.

➢ Pour milk into the pot and put it on the stove on medium heat. You have to heat the milk to 180°F. Use the thermometer regularly to ensure the milk's temperature doesn't exceed that level. Keep stirring the milk constantly.

➢ Once the milk has reached that temperature, remove the pot from the stove. You have to let the milk cool to 110°F. You can either place the milk on the counter then wait for it to cool, or make an ice bath in the sink and put the pot in it. Keep checking the temperature so that it is exactly at 110°F.

➢ After the milk has cooled, pour the yogurt into the pot. Whisk the yogurt and milk so they combine properly. Make sure the two ingredients are thoroughly mixed, or else keep on whisking till they do.

➢ Pour the contents of the pot into the jars. Use two or three jars, as per your requirement. From experience, I can say that the two quart-sized jars should be enough. If that isn't the case, simply pour the remaining mixture into the other jar. After the milk and yogurt have been completely transferred to the jars, put their lids on. Make sure the containers are completely airtight and there is no chance of the mixture coming out.

➢ Then, put the jars into the cooler. Fill the cooler up with water till the jars are nearly submerged, almost up to the lids. Don't fill to the brim as the water might seep into the mixture through the lid. The temperature of the water has to be precisely 120°F. The thermometer will again come into play.

➤ Find a spot where no one will disturb the cooler. Close the lid and then keep it there for six hours. This is known as the 'incubation' period and is the distinct feature of the process of making Greek yogurt. The purpose of the incubation period is to speed up the culturing process. The cultures start taking effect, making the yogurt healthy and nutritious.

➤ Once the six-hour incubation is complete, move the containers from the cooler to the fridge. Here too you have to keep the containers for six hours. This is done so that the culturing can stop and the yogurt achieves its desired texture and taste.

➤ After six hours, remove the containers from the fridge. The yogurt is ready and in an edible state but is not Greek yogurt as of yet. There is one final step, perhaps the most important one of all: straining. To strain the yogurt, you will use the mesh strainer. You will need a bowl for this. You can use the pot you used earlier for the initial steps.

➤ Next, take the cheese cloth and line it along the sides of the bowl (or any vessel you use). It is better to double the layer to ensure the yogurt doesn't seep out. Then, you have to spoon the yogurt on to the strainer. Leave it as it is for a couple of hours so that it drains out. You can let it stay longer if you feel the yogurt is not thick enough after two hours.

After straining, your Greek yogurt is prepared and ready to eat. You can eat it right after removing it from the strainer and putting it in a container.

As you can see, the entire recipe to make Greek yogurt takes around 15 hours. However, the actual preparation and work that you have to do hardly takes more than an hour. You only have to make sure you are alert and put the containers in the cooler and fridge at the right time, as well as straining the mixture.

When considering the health benefits of Greek yogurt, it is superior to most other types of yogurt. In fact, it won't be wrong to say that it is one of the healthiest dairy products you can make at home and eat. Add to that the ease of making it and it becomes an even more enticing option.

In the case of Greek yogurt, you cannot even complain about the taste. The taste is customizable and you have a wide range of flavours to choose from. It all comes down to how you want to use this recipe. The steps have to be followed in the exact order but that is the only restriction.

So, if you have heard good things about this superfood, it is time you try it as well.

Yogurt Parfait

Yogurt parfait is a breakfast meal. It usually contains common breakfast food choices like granola, berries, fruits, etc, along with yogurt. It possesses great taste, you can modify the ingredients any way you want, and it is incredibly healthy. So, there is no reason for you to not try yogurt parfait.

One of the best things about yogurt parfait is its taste and texture. You can get your children to eat it every day for breakfast, which will take care of their daily nutritional needs. If you feel they are not too inclined towards eating healthier breakfast items, it won't take much convincing to get them to eat yogurt parfait.

Image Link:
http://www.flickr.com/photos/mentalize/6168924711/

The way the parfait is made gives it a rich texture and appearance. There are several layers of yogurt, each containing fruits and nuts. You can also throw in some raw honey and granola to add to the taste and nutritional value of your breakfast dish. And it doesn't contain many calories either.

Benefits of Eating Yogurt Parfait

There is no dearth of yogurt-based food items, for instance yogurt smoothies, ice creams and plain yogurt itself. Yet, you wouldn't eat any of those for breakfast, would you? Nutritionists have proven that breakfast is the most important meal of the day and it is important to make sure that it is healthy and nutritious.

Healthy & Tasty

You can enjoy the various benefits provided by yogurt but without having to put up with the tangy, salty taste of plain yogurt. Instead, you have blueberries, bananas, strawberries, kiwis, etc, adding their flavour to the parfait. It makes it palatable for you to start off your day on a healthy note.

Nutritional Benefits

Of course, one should not ignore the nutritional benefits provided by a single serving of yogurt parfait. Based on the typical ingredients used, you can get a fair share of your recommended daily dose of calcium and protein from yogurt parfait. Also, it is rich in probiotics that improve your metabolism and digestion.

Variety of Ingredients

You can choose fruits that are highly nutritious, such as apples, kiwis, etc, apart from tasting healthy. Moreover, there are numerous options as far as the grain to sprinkle on top of the parfait is concerned. Granola remains the most popular option, by far, but you can use oatmeal or cereal. In fact, crushed bran cookies or crackers aren't too bad either.

Flexibility

Plus, you have the option to customize yogurt parfait any which way you want. It is not like you are ordering it at a restaurant and have to go with what's available. When making parfait at home, yogurt is the only constant. You can change everything else, from the fruit to the grain, even the size of the serving, without a negative impact.

Boost Nutrition

As if yogurt parfait isn't healthy enough, you can actually boost its nutritional value by adding raw honey to the recipe. You can either ladle it on top or have it somewhere between the layers of yogurt. Also, you can sprinkle cinnamon on the parfait before eating it.

A Full Meal

Talking purely about the ingredients being used and their inherent nutritional value, it wouldn't be wrong to say that yogurt parfait is a full meal. Though it has been traditionally reserved for breakfast, this nutritious dish can be eaten at any time of day or night. There is little chance you will want to eat anything else right after it.

As you can see, there are numerous benefits of eating yogurt parfait. We will go over the steps you need to follow to make it in the convenience of your home.

Ingredients

Before going over the recipe one step at a time, it is ideal to check out the ingredients used to make yogurt parfait. These include:

o Granola
o Cereal (if you want)
o 1 cup yogurt (plain, frozen, Greek, anything)
o Fruits & Berries

You can be flexible with the ingredients, provided you get the taste and nutritional value you are looking for. You also have the option to choose any type of yogurt you want. If you feel plain yogurt is too tangy, you can use flavoured yogurt instead. This will add to the parfait's taste for sure.

The equipment and supplies you need to make yogurt parfait at home are also limited. You only need a spoon, a spatula and a kitchen cloth. Plus, you need to have a glass or a bowl in which you make and serve parfait. This is about as far as it gets with ingredients and equipment required for homemade yogurt parfait.

Tips & Tricks

One very important thing you need to remember when making yogurt parfait is that the ingredients are not to be stirred at any stage. Of course the recipe requires you to use the ingredients with each other, but it doesn't mean you have to stir them or blend them.

Also, you can make your parfait healthier by forgoing the use of sugar and adding raw honey or any other sweet yet healthy fruit. It depends purely on your preference how sweet you want the yogurt parfait to be. In fact, if you can get your hands on some healthy cookies, don't hesitate to break and sprinkle them over the parfait.

Parfait is best served in a bowl but there is no hard and fast rule regarding that. You can choose to eat it in a glass or plate, with any utensil you want. The key is to get a solid serving so that you can enjoy the benefits it delivers.

There is no restriction as far as the berries and fruits are concerned. You can choose any one/s you want. From peaches to bananas, the options are endless.

Recipe

Coming to the business end of things, here is the step by step process you have to follow to make yogurt parfait.

- ➤ The first step is not directly related to the recipe but for the purpose of making things easier for you. Since the ingredients used to make parfait are varied and have to be prepared separately, keep them at hand so you don't have to wander off once you have started making the parfait. Organize them in a way that they are easily accessible.
- ➤ Take a large bowl or glass. Choose wisely so the ingredients can fit into it. Before you put the ingredients in, keep the container in the fridge for a few minutes. This ensures the container is cool before you use it and it helps keep the ingredients cool.
- ➤ Pour ¼ cup yogurt into the glass. Make sure you don't pour more than that as you have to leave room for other ingredients.

➤ Add other ingredients to the yogurt in the bowl. You don't have to mix or whisk the ingredients just yet. Simply put them into the bowl with the yogurt and then move on to the next step.

➤ Pour the remaining ¾ cup of yogurt into the bowl. This is a useful trick to know when making yogurt parfait. You have to make sure the yogurt is layered such that there is more on top than below the ingredients. Or else, the ingredients get soaked by the yogurt and become soggy which makes them less palatable.

Your parfait is ready! That is it. This is perhaps the most convenient of all yogurt recipes you can try at home, not to forget that it is incredibly healthy.

Things to Remember

There are a couple of things you have to keep in mind when making yogurt parfait. One of them is mentioned above, that the yogurt has to be divided in such a way that more of it is on top of the ingredients.

Also, make sure the yogurt and other ingredients are absolutely fresh. There is no other way you can be sure that the parfait's taste will come out the way you want it to be.

A golden tip to keep in mind is regarding the parfait's flavour. Like I said before, you can choose any fruits and berries you want. If you want to amplify the taste of the fruits and berries, it is better to use plain yogurt.

On the other hand, you can use flavoured yogurt. Before you use it, check the ingredients carefully to make sure there are active cultures in it. Only then will it deliver the benefits you are looking for.

In case you are using flavoured yogurt, choose the other ingredients accordingly. For instance, if you are using strawberry flavoured yogurt, it wouldn't make sense to add fresh strawberries.

As far as serving parfait is concerned, it is better to eat it right after you prepare it. The longer you keep it, the more the risk of the granola or cereal getting soggy. When soggy, they lose their taste as well as their crunchy and crispy texture.

So, yogurt parfait is, by far, one of the easiest dairy products for you to make. You don't need to cook or bake. Simply put the ingredients in one place and that's it.

Vanilla Yogurt

Vanilla is one of the most popular flavours of yogurt. Though berries take precedence, vanilla yogurt is widely consumed and its sales can be compared to that of vanilla ice cream. Commercial vanilla yogurt is made using artificial sweeteners and other preservatives.

Making vanilla yogurt at home can make it very healthy and nutritious. We have gone over the health benefits of yogurt. By making your own vanilla yogurt, you get to enjoy the health benefits of natural vanilla as well. So, you double the goodness without having to compromise on the flavour.

You may be surprised at how easy it is to make vanilla yogurt at home. Given the premium prices charged by the leading flavoured yogurt brands in the market, one assumes making it is a difficult task, when in fact it is not. Provided you follow the recipe step by step, you shouldn't have any trouble getting it right the first time.

Health Benefits of Vanilla Yogurt

Homemade vanilla yogurt retains the active cultures of yogurt so you get to enjoy all the health benefits we have gone over in the first couple of chapters. What you get in addition are the benefits of eating vanilla. This is why you are recommended to make your own vanilla yogurt using natural vanilla extract.

Here are some of the benefits of eating vanilla yogurt:

Relieves Anxiety and Tension

Stress is a part of the modern lifestyle. It is difficult to escape stress for the average person. From job insecurity to relationship issues, there are many stress triggers, any of which can cause you to feel anxious and tense. Anxiety affects your physical and mental health while also making it hard for you to fulfil your responsibilities. Well, you can kiss anxiety goodbye by adding vanilla yogurt to your diet. For over four centuries now, vanilla has been considered a healthy relaxant. In fact, it was used for sedation in Europe during the 1600s.

Fight Claustrophobia

There is no conclusive evidence to support this but eating vanilla has been known to reduce the symptoms and effects of claustrophobia. Initially, vanilla was used to carry out aromatherapy which helped patients get rid of their claustrophobia. Eating natural yogurt can also help them, though not to the extent that aromatherapy does.

Fights Free Radicals & Toxins

Like stress, free radicals and toxins are also a part of the modern lifestyle. With the rising levels of pollution and the unhealthy dietary choices people make, it becomes difficult for the body to fight off these free radicals. They can cause cell damage and make you look older than you are. Obviously, that is something no one wants. Vanilla yogurt can help your body fight free radicals and toxins as vanilla has anti-oxidative properties.

Prevents Cancer

Vanilla yogurt can also help prevent certain types of cancer. Vanilla has anti-carcinogenic properties that fight cancer cells and halt the growth of cancerous tumours. Its ability to fight free radicals also contributes towards its anti-cancer properties.

Aids Weight Loss

Vanilla bean or extract can also aid weight loss efforts. However, that is not true of commercial vanilla yogurt, which is full of sugar. Vanilla yogurt made using natural vanilla extract can help you lose weight quickly and in a healthy and safe manner.

These are just some of the benefits you can enjoy by making vanilla yogurt at home and eating it regularly. The key is to use natural vanilla beans or extract so that the nutrients are present in their organic form.

Apart from the health benefits, a distinct advantage of vanilla yogurt is that it can replace dessert. Instead of eating cakes and pies with high calorie content, you should eat a cup of homemade vanilla yogurt after dinner. It will soothe your sweet tooth while ensuring you don't pile on the pounds.

Supplies & Equipment

You don't need a lot of supplies to make vanilla yogurt. In fact, you only need a bowl and a pot for the entire recipe. The pot is used to heat the milk on the stove and the bowl for mixing all the ingredients. You will have to use something to whip and whisk the ingredients. There are no restrictions on what you use.

It is also a good idea to have a thermometer at hand. Though you can easily guess the temperature of the milk and other ingredients, using a thermometer makes the entire process more accurate. This way, you are less likely to make a mistake and can get it right the very first time.

I am sure it won't take you more than a few minutes to have all the supplies you need ready and prepared to start cooking some vanilla yogurt.

Ingredients

Vanilla yogurt, or any flavoured yogurt for that matter, is dependent hugely on its ingredients. You have to ensure you get the quantities right or else you don't get the taste and texture you are looking for. Healthy though it may not be, but commercial yogurt is tasty and has a wonderful texture. That is something you can achieve when making vanilla yogurt at home but you have to follow the recipe closely.

For the recipe, you need 4 cups of milk. With milk, you can choose from raw milk, whole milk and low-fat milk. There are no restrictions but it is better to go for a healthy variant rather than just selecting any one at random. Also, keep in mind that the pot/pan you use for the recipe is big enough for 4 cups of milk.

You will also require powdered milk along with liquid milk. Get ½ cup of dry milk which will be added to the recipe later on. For sweetening the recipe, you can use brown sugar, which provides the taste but without the health hazards that come with sugar. You will have to add at least 4 to 6 teaspoons of brown sugar.

A great substitute for sugar is raw honey. Raw honey is healthy, nutritious and will only add to the natural wholesomeness of the vanilla yogurt you make. The only potential drawback is that it may override the taste of the vanilla. You can get around that by adding a teaspoon at a time and tasting the yogurt till you get the perfect flavour.

Next is the yogurt starter. The starter has to contain active cultures. You will need ½ cup of this as well. Double check to ensure the ingredients include active cultures or else the vanilla yogurt's benefits are compromised.

Last, but not the least, is the vanilla. Now, here you have a couple of options to choose from. You can go for artificial vanilla flavouring (something I would not recommend). It will lend the yogurt the flavour you are looking for and might prove to be tastier than natural vanilla. But this does mean you have to forgo the benefits of vanilla yogurt.

The ideal option is to use natural vanilla extract. It is easily available in the market and you only need to look at the ingredients to see that it is completely natural and has not been processed in any way whatsoever. The flavour may not be as exquisite as you get when you use artificial vanilla flavouring but it will provide the benefits you are looking for. Of course, you can balance the flavour with the brown sugar or honey.

You don't require more than 1 tablespoon of natural vanilla extract for the recipe. Get the ingredients ready before you get to the preparation phase.

Recipe

Vanilla yogurt is a recipe in which you don't actually have to 'cook' anything. All you are required to do is bring the ingredients into the state they should be in for the recipe and that is all. It won't take you more than a few minutes to do so.

However, you will have to keep the yogurt aside for a few hours at a time, during which you can even complete your work shift and come back home to find your vanilla yogurt ready.

The recipe is described below, step by step, to make it easy for you to follow.

> First, put the yogurt starter in a bowl and leave it out on the counter. Make sure you select a spot that

is not damp or cool. You have to warm the starter, not cool it. Keep it out till it comes to room temperature. Use the thermometer if you aren't sure. Complete this step before you start to prepare the milk.

➢ Pour the milk into the pot or saucepan and put it on the stove on medium heat. Make sure you don't turn the heat up as you don't want the milk to boil over or get stuck to the bottom of the pan. That will make it unusable for the purpose of the recipe and you will have to discard it. Bring it to a boil but turn the stove off just before it starts rising. It won't take more than 10 minutes.

➢ Then, you have to take the pot off the stove and let the milk cool. It also has to come down to room temperature, which may take some time. You can leave it out on the counter and wait for it cool.

➢ If you want to speed things up, make an ice bath in the sink, about which you read in the previous couple of chapters, and place the pot in it. Make sure you keep checking the temperature to ensure it doesn't cool down too much.

➢ Once the milk has reached the desired temperature, you have to add all the ingredients except the starter. This means putting in the vanilla extract, dry milk and whichever sweetening agent you want to use. Whip in the ingredients so they really combine with the milk. Keep stirring till you are absolutely sure the ingredients are part of the milk.

➢ Now you have to put the yogurt starter into the milk. The starter also has to be mixed in properly so keep stirring until it does. However, do not whip the mixture as it interferes with the proper combining of the ingredients. They have to be mixed well but without whisking or whipping.

The 'active' part of the recipe is now complete. You have combined all the ingredients and they are in the perfect state they should be for you to make delicious and healthy vanilla yogurt. As with all other types of yogurt we have covered in this book so far, you have to let the yogurt stand for some time.

- ➤ The yogurt starter, particularly the active bacteria, needs some time to take hold and get the yogurt into its final shape. This is why you have to keep it aside for some time. For this, pour the mixture you have made into a bowl and cover it with cloth. Keep it in a place where you are certain no one will tamper with it. You have to let it be for at least 12 hours. This is why I suggest you make the mixture in the morning before leaving for work.

- ➤ The longer you keep the yogurt out for, the firmer and tarter it becomes. After 12 hours have gone by, you can check the taste and texture to decide whether you need to keep it for longer or you have achieved the desired flavour.

- ➤ When you are confident that the vanilla yogurt is ready and you don't need to 'cook' it any further, transfer it to a container and place it in the fridge for a couple of hours. Around 4 hours are enough for the culturing process to stop and the yogurt to firm up.

Once 4 hours go by, take the vanilla yogurt out from the fridge and start eating. You can store it for up to two weeks without worrying about it getting spoiled. As long as you keep it in a container with the lid tightly on, there shouldn't be any risk of it getting spoiled whatsoever.

There is little chance you would want to store your vanilla yogurt for long given its wonderful taste. It is recommended that you eat at least one serving a day to make the most of the nutritional benefits it provides. It wouldn't be a bad idea to make vanilla yogurt a part of your daily diet.

Coconut Yogurt

Coconut is one of the healthiest fruits around. A number of food items produced using raw coconuts are consumed the world over on a daily basis. It is probable that you have used coconut oil, coconut milk or coconut water at least once.

Coconut possesses vital nutrients and minerals your body needs, plus providing a host of other health benefits. Coconut yogurt may not be the most popular flavour in fruit yogurt but health enthusiasts know that there is no better fruit to add to homemade yogurt than coconut.

Plus, it is easy to make and will improve your health. There is no reason for you to not give it a go. Not to forget that coconut yogurt is quite tasty as well.

Benefits of Coconut Yogurt

Coconut yogurt is one of the best types of yogurts you can make at home and eat regularly. You might be surprised to learn that in certain aspects, it is superior even to Greek yogurt, which is considered the best of the lot. Let's look at some of the benefits of this delicacy.

Source of Healthy Calories

Though calories are made out to be the antagonists when it comes to weight gain, it is true that your body needs a certain amount of calories to function properly. The main purpose of calories is to provide the energy your body needs to get through the day. Coconut yogurt has the perfect quantity of calories for you to eat as part of your breakfast.

A single serving will provide around 150 to 250 calories, depending on the serving size and ingredients. This is actually less calories than Greek yogurt. If you are feeling tired and drained over the course of a day, it is a good idea to make coconut yogurt a part of breakfast. It will help you start your day on the right note and ensure you have plenty of energy to fulfil all your responsibilities.

You can even add cereal, fruit and other breakfast items to make the yogurt healthier. The ingredients and recipe will be discussed in the next part of this chapter.

Dairy for Vegans

Believe it or not, coconut yogurt is a dairy product for vegans. A minor tweak to the recipe ensures that coconut yogurt ceases to be a dairy product yet you get to enjoy the taste, texture and health benefits of yogurt. This makes it a perfect recipe for vegans to follow. Their ideology may not allow them to eat any dairy products but this one could be the exception.

Perfect for the Lactose Intolerant

Since it is not a dairy product per se, coconut yogurt can be eaten safely and without risk by people suffering from lactose intolerance. The secret behind this is to use coconut milk instead of any of the regular options. This ensures there is no lactose in the coconut yogurt and you can eat it without fear or worry.

Get a Vitamin Boost

Coconut yogurt serves a number of vital vitamins for your body. According to the nutritional qualities of a single serving of homemade coconut yogurt, you can get up to 15% of your daily recommended intake for vitamin A and 4% vitamin C. Vitamin A, in particular, is extremely important as it helps preserve your eyesight and keeps it in perfect shape. The risk of your vision getting weaker is reduced. Plus, the membranes and skin around your eyes stay healthy.

An Additional Energy Boost

The energy you get through a bowl of coconut yogurt does not stop with the calories. In addition, your body also receives carbohydrates and protein, both of which are converted to energy by your body. You can easily get up to 11% of the carbohydrates you need daily with coconut yogurt.

Helps Build Muscle

Coconut yogurt can also help you build muscle as it contains iron as well. Up to 10% of your daily recommended intake of iron can come from a single serving of coconut yogurt. If you are into body building, you will find coconut yogurt a wonderful natural supplement to boost your weightlifting routine.

Preserves Your Teeth

Coconut yogurt can help protect your teeth and prevent dental problems. Over time, tooth decay can set in, causing pain and discomfort and also leading to the risk of losing your teeth. Eating coconut yogurt can preserve your teeth in their natural form and ensure that you don't face any such problems.

Improves Metabolism

Coconut itself is great for your metabolism and so is yogurt. Combine the two and the effect is compounded. Your body absorbs nutrients better once you start eating coconut yogurt regularly. Not to mention the fact that coconut yogurt itself contains a host of nutrients for you to enjoy. This will also help you lose weight quickly.

Healthier Hair and Skin

Coconut yogurt is not only great for your health but also does wonders for your appearance. Your hair and skin get better when you start eating coconut yogurt. After all, there is a reason why people apply coconut oil to their hair and skin. Your hair grows stronger, thicker and shinier with the risk of hair loss at a minimum. Moreover, your skin gets healthy, fighting off signs of aging and you start looking younger.

Reduces Inflammation

Coconut yogurt contains anti-inflammatory properties which reduce inflammation. If you are suffering from irritation because of haemorrhoids or any other disorder related to the bowels, start eating coconut yogurt right away. It will have you feeling better in no time at all.

These are just some of the health benefits of coconut yogurt. In a way, you can say that this is just the tip of the iceberg. There are a host of other benefits your body can get through coconut yogurt.

Ingredients & Supplies

There are a couple of ways you can make coconut yogurt at home. Each is effective and you have complete freedom to choose either. The key is to follow the recipe to the letter and have the right ingredients on hand for it.

Depending on which recipe you follow, you will require coconut meat, coconut water, coconut kefir, yogurt starter, arrowroot and coconut milk.

What I would recommend is that you try both recipes once and then decide which one you find easier or the one that delivers the better results.

For the first recipe, the ingredients you need are:

- 800ml coconut milk
- 1 tablespoon arrowroot
- 3 tablespoons yogurt starter with active cultures

The supplies you require for this recipe are:

- Containers (you need enough storage space for 800ml yogurt)
- A slow cooker or thermometer
- A saucepan
- A mug
- A spoon

For the other recipe, the required ingredients are:

- 1 tablespoon coconut kefir
- ½ cup raw coconut water
- 1 tablespoon yogurt starter with active cultures
- 1 tablespoon vanilla bean
- 2 cups coconut meat

For this recipe, you need to have a blender or food processor on hand. Also, you will require cheese cloth and a couple of jars to store yogurt during the fermentation process.

Recipes

As mentioned above, there are two different recipes which can be used to make coconut yogurt at home. You can try one and if it works, stick to it. Or else you can give both of them a go and decide which one you prefer. Either way, you will need to know the steps for the recipe.

We will start with the second recipe, i.e. the recipe for which the ingredients and supplies were mentioned second in the previous part (coconut kefir, water, meat, etc). This recipe is quite simple and doesn't take much time or effort.

> ➢ The first step is to put all the ingredients (coconut meat, coconut water, coconut kefir, vanilla bean, and starter) into the blender or food processor.
> ➢ Turn the blender on and blend the ingredients till they form a smooth, creamy mixture. Make sure there aren't any chunks of coconut meat and that all the ingredients have been thoroughly mixed.
> ➢ Pour out the contents of the blender into a container. Cover the container with cheese cloth and let it stay for 12 hours. The container has to be kept at room temperature so select a spot accordingly. Don't put the container in a cold, damp or warm place.
> ➢ After 12 hours have elapsed, move the container to your fridge. There, you have to keep it for a whole day, 24 hours. Even though it may not take more than a few minutes for you to process the ingredients and prepare the mixture, you have to keep the yogurt for 36 hours before it comes to its final shape.

If everything goes according to plan, the coconut yogurt, at this point, has a tangy smell and a sweet & sour taste. You can start eating it right away. This is the dairy-free version of coconut yogurt so you cannot expect it to be as tasty as regular coconut yogurt.

However, you can improve the taste by adding fruits to the yogurt. An even better option is to create a 'crumble' and put into the yogurt.

The crumble is made using dates, almonds, cinnamon and walnuts. You only need a handful of each. Toss the dates into the blender and crush them till they become tiny chunks. Then, add the remaining ingredients and keep blending till they become almost flour-like. It is at this point that you can add them to the yogurt and mix them in. This is the first recipe for coconut yogurt you can follow. It is healthier but the flavour itself might be an issue for you. If you don't find it to your liking, you can follow the second recipe laid out below.

➤ Pour coconut milk into the saucepan. Put it over the stove on medium heat. You have to heat the milk up to 185°F. Make sure the milk doesn't boil. Use the thermometer to measure the temperature and check whether it is at the desired level. The heat will kill any bacteria present in the coconut milk, ensuring the bacteria in the yogurt starter can take effect immediately.

➤ Remove the saucepan from the stove and place it in a cool place. You have to bring the milk's temperature down to 113°F before you can proceed to the next step. Once again, you can speed up the process by preparing an ice bath for the saucepan.

➤ Take a mug and put in the other two ingredients, the yogurt starter and the arrowroot. Then, use a spoon to pour a couple of spoonfuls of milk into the mug. Mix them together and then pour into the saucepan. Keep mixing till the ingredients combine properly.

➤ Pour the saucepan's contents into the containers and seal them off. Keep them aside for a minimum of 12 hours. This is the incubation period. The longer you let the yogurt stand, the more pronounced its flavour is. If you get the perfect flavour, note the time it took and stick to it in the future.

> The last step is putting the containers in the fridge for a few hours. This is done so the cultures finally die. They are responsible for thickening the yogurt and if allowed to do their thing, they will make the yogurt too thick for you to eat. Putting it in the fridge for 3 to 4 hours should do the trick.

Your coconut yogurt is ready for you to enjoy. You can tuck in right away. A golden tip for you in case the yogurt isn't thick enough is to add more arrowroot the next time you make it. The batch you already made cannot be made thicker after it is prepared and ready to eat. This is one risk you have to bear.

As you can see, both recipes to make coconut yogurt are straightforward and quite easy to follow. You only need to follow the steps and there is little chance anything will go wrong. It does take some time for the yogurt to come into its final form but it is worth the wait.

I suggest you make a large quantity of coconut yogurt at once. When you start eating it, you will find it hard to stop. It is quite possible the first batch runs out in no time!

Yogurt Dip

What is your favourite dip? It is likely that you haven't tried yogurt dips till now. The exotic and spicy dips have grown quite popular over the years and are a staple of a get-together, particularly when watching a game on TV. I can say, with confidence, that yogurt dips are a better option than any other dip you try.

Image Link:
http://www.flickr.com/photos/copyright1972/7085310847/

Plus, you can easily make it at home. You don't need to spend hours and hours on it. The recipe is simple and clearly laid out. All you have to do is get the ingredients and then prepare them accordingly. It won't be too much of a pain. The taste will make it worth your while to indulge in yogurt dip.

Benefits

There are numerous benefits of yogurt dip. For one, it is made from fresh yogurt with active cultures so you can enjoy the various benefits it provides. Health is probably the last thing on one's mind when thinking about which dip to choose. Yogurt dips allow you to bridge the gap.

Apart from the yogurt, the ingredients you use also lend their particular nutritional qualities to the dip. This goes for any vegetables or fruits you may choose to have in the dip. There are virtually no restrictions. Just follow the recipe and change the ingredients as per your preference.

Health benefits aside, there are a few other advantages of yogurt dip as well:

Customizable Ingredients

You can choose any ingredient you want for the dip. The yogurt remains but other ingredients can be customized any way you want. It depends on the type of flavour you want to get from the dip. For a 'cool' flavour, herbs are a great option. If you are in the mood for something spicy, adding chillies to the dip will do the trick. Same goes for fruits as well. You can go for the more staid ones or sweet ones, based on what you are looking for.

Sweet or Savoury

The flavour can be sweet or savoury. As mentioned above, the ingredients can be changed around to achieve the flavour you are looking for. It is the simple matter of combining the ingredients in a perfect way to get the perfect taste. Aside from that, there is nothing really stopping you from experimenting with the flavour of yogurt dip you make. This is perhaps the biggest advantage you get by making yogurt dip over any other commercially available dip.

Takes No Time!

The recipe itself takes no time to make. You only need to prepare the ingredients and toss them into the food processor. That is all you have to do. How long can that take? Making yogurt dip is not like the other yogurt recipes we have gone over in this book in which you have to keep the mixture aside for 12 hours or more. Here, the active time is the total time to get the item ready to eat.

Easy As Pie!

Of course, you aren't baking a pie but making yogurt dip is as easy as pie. This is the reason why it takes virtually no time for you to prepare the dip and serve it. In fact, I would say it is more convenient for you to make your dip at home than running to the supermarket to buy it.

Tastes Better

Do you think I would suggest a recipe if it didn't possess superior taste to the available alternatives? This is the case with yogurt dip as well. Exotic as it may be, yogurt dip easily takes the cake when it comes to taste. Add to that the health advantages and you have every reason to give yogurt dip a try.

Costs Less

How expensive can it be to buy dip? However, why should you spend that much money when you can easily make better dip that costs less. The only cost you have to bear is for the yogurt and ingredients. Compare that to the cost of average dip, the difference is considerable.

Absolute Control

When making your own yogurt dip, you get to choose everything, from the base to the final topping. You have absolute control over the process and can chop and change it any way you want. The other option is to go with what manufacturers offer. There, you don't have much leverage in terms of choosing the taste and ingredients.

There is no dearth of reasons for you to try yogurt dip. The fact that it is easy to make at home sweetens the deal.

Supplies & Equipment

To make delicious yogurt dip at home, you will need a blender or a food processor. The ingredients have to be mixed very well. You will also need a bowl in which the ingredients will be poured after being thoroughly blended for mixing.

You will also need a spoon or fork to mix the ingredients once they have been processed. The only other utensils you will require are for cutting the vegetables and fruit. In other words, you don't need to get something special to make yogurt. In all likelihood, the equipment and supplies you need are already in your home.

Ingredients

The ingredients will vary based on the type of yogurt dip you want. From avocado to zucchini, you can choose any fruit and vegetable you want. Keeping in mind the taste considerations, it is better to overlook some fruits and vegetables which aren't palatable (I'm sure you know the ones I am talking about).

One thing that remains constant is yogurt. You have to use yogurt with active cultures. Here again you have complete freedom to choose any type of yogurt you want. From plain yogurt to Greek yogurt to flavoured yogurt, you can select any type of yogurt you feel like using.

The only thing you should aim for is to get fat-free yogurt. Feel free to digress, as it is unlikely the presence of a little fat will compromise the health benefits of yogurt dip. The recipes you learned in previous chapters will come in handy here. You can make your own yogurt and then use it to make yogurt dip.

This gives you absolute control over the entire process. You don't have to rely on the ingredients and processes used by big brands to make their yogurt dip. This way, you get to make your dip the way you want it to be.

A great tip you can follow is to use flavoured yogurt for the base of the yogurt dip. This way, you can mix and match different flavours without having to add too many ingredients to the recipe. For instance, you can mix strawberry flavoured yogurt and add bananas on top. There is no limit to your creativity and imagination in terms of the ingredients you want to use.

The quantity of the yogurt to make the dip depends on how much of it you want to make at a time. If you are trying it for the first time, it is better to use ¼ cup. This is an ample quantity to make yogurt dip. Check the taste and texture to decide whether or not you got it right. If you did, simply increase the quantity and make again.

You can also store yogurt dip in the fridge, provided you use a sealed container. It will stay fresh and edible for at least a week.

Recipe

Prepare all the ingredients the way they are intended to be used in the recipe. If you are using vegetables, you have to dice and square it into small pieces. In the case of herbs, chop them to tiny strands. This makes it easier for the ingredients to mix together properly which is essential for great yogurt dip.

The other thing is regarding the yogurt. You can use any type of yogurt but do make sure it is ready to use. Otherwise you will have to wait for the yogurt to get ready before you can start making the dip.

Follow the steps listed below to make yogurt dip:

> Prepare all the ingredients. Put them into the blender or food processor and turn it on. You have to blend them till they are thoroughly chopped up. There shouldn't be any solid pieces or chunks. They don't go well in the dip.

> Once the ingredients have been thoroughly processed, shift them from the blender/food processor into a bowl. Pour the yogurt into the bowl with the ingredients.

> Use a spoon or fork and mix the ingredients with the yogurt. Don't whisk too hard as that may disturb the yogurt's thickness. You can also stir the ingredients.

Regardless of the method you use, make sure the ingredients and yogurt mix well.

This is pretty much it as far as making yogurt dip is concerned. You might be surprised at how easy the recipe actually is. As long as you stick to the recipe, there is no reason why making yogurt dip at home should be a problem for you.

See, I wasn't wrong when I said making yogurt dip is easy. You can use it as an appetizer on its own or use it as a side dish with dinner. Get the crackers and crisps out and start dipping!

Yogurt Juice

Here is something you might not have heard too much about: yogurt juice. There are many ways you can eat yogurt but when it comes to liquid, smoothies are pretty much all you have. If you aren't in the mood for a smoothie, yet want to drink yogurt, you can make your own yogurt juice.

Drinkable yogurt is available in the market but it is too expensive. And when you go over the recipe, you will realize that you are paying the company for doing virtually nothing. You are better off learning the recipe and making it at home. It takes hardly a few minutes to prepare yogurt juice.

Benefits of Yogurt Juice

For one, you don't have to eat yogurt. If you aren't a fan of eating yogurt, drinking yogurt juice is a convenient option. The nutrition you derive from yogurt remains intact. This makes it a wonderful substitute for breakfast. Drink a glass of yogurt juice and you are good to go.

To make yogurt juice, you only need to toss some ingredients into the blender and then process them. There is no preparation phase or anything else. It helps that the ingredients are ready to use. I would recommend that you prepare the ingredients at home.

It will only take 5 minutes for you to make yogurt juice. Surely, that is less time than it takes for you to go to the nearest store which sells drinkable yogurt.

Supplies & Equipment

To prepare yogurt juice, the only equipment you need is a blender. You have to blend the ingredients to make juice, so a blender is the ideal equipment for it. Apart from this, you need to have glasses to drink the juice and bottles or any containers to keep it in the fridge.

Ingredients

To make yogurt juice, you need 2 cups of plain yogurt. Though there is no restriction on the type of yogurt you use, I would recommend you use plain yogurt. Since you are making juice, it is better to have the flavour of the juice take precedence over the type of yogurt you use.

This brings me to the most important part: fruit juice. For this recipe, you need to have a glass of fruit juice. Though buying the commercial variant is more convenient, it is better to stick to the spirit of homemade yogurt and make it at home. After all, it doesn't take much effort to squeeze a couple of oranges or cut and toss apples in the juicer.

It is up to you to decide which type of juice you want to use. You are the one who has to make it. In fact, it wouldn't be too bad to buy commercial fruit juice. Just make sure the one you buy is natural and has few, if any preservatives. That gives you more flexibility in terms of the flavours you can select.

The third ingredient is water. Water is to make the yogurt 'liquid' and allow the juice and the yogurt to combine properly. You can also add ice cubes if you want. You can even use two different juices.

Recipe

There is no such 'recipe' per se. You simply have to put all the ingredients inside the blender and then press the 'on' button. Keep blending till you are sure the ingredients are mixed properly. After that, pour the juice from the blender into the bottle or container you have set aside to store it.

It is a good idea to keep the juice in the fridge for a few hours before you drink it. Not only does this chill it up but the ingredients settle and the taste is more pronounced. You will really enjoy drinking it after it has been in the fridge for a couple of hours.

However, don't forget to shake the container before you pour the juice into a glass. This will ensure the ingredients aren't separate. The yogurt juice's ingredients have the tendency to do that once kept in the fridge. You can tweak the ingredients to increase or reduce the juice's thickness.

To thicken it, add some yogurt and to reduce the thickness, add more water to the recipe. It's not too hard, is it?

Yogurt Shake

Yogurt shake is similar to milk shake, the only difference being that you replace one dairy ingredient with another. Instead of using milk to prepare the shake, you have to pour yogurt into the blender.

Milk shakes remain a popular drink, consumed by people of all ages around the world. Fruit shakes in particular are in high demand and most people make them at home. If you have made milk shake before, making yogurt shake at home shouldn't be a hassle for you. The recipe and the process you have to follow to make yogurt shake is similar to that for milk shake.

Image Link:
http://www.flickr.com/photos/ozten/3166845211/

As I have pointed out on a couple of occasions, homemade yogurt is healthier than milk. Even though milk shakes are healthy and nutritious, yogurt shakes are superior. This is due to the simple fact that the yogurt you use has active cultures.

Once you start making yogurt shakes, you will find them irresistible. The frothy, smooth texture of the beverage combined with the wonderful taste is simply too good to be true. You will be licking your lips and enjoying the flavour long after you are done drinking it.

Supplies & Equipment

I don't even need to list the equipment and supplies for you. All you have to use is your blender. That is pretty much it. The ingredients will determine the yogurt shake's taste so make sure you choose the ones you like.

Ingredients

To make two glasses of yogurt shake, you need at least 1 cup of yogurt. Modify the quantity of the yogurt based on your observation. It is better to use homemade yogurt, flavoured or plain. The active cultures will really boost the yogurt shake's nutritional value.

A small tip regarding flavoured yogurt is that it can complement the taste of the fruit you are using to make the shake. For instance, you can combine pineapple yogurt with strawberries and bananas to create an exotic and unique yogurt shake flavour. Since the list of flavours is virtually endless, choose any you want.

Coming back to the ingredients, you only need to add fruits. The fruits you use depend on your preference. You can opt for fruits that are more nutritious or which taste better. Since there are no restrictions, feel free to indulge.

One thing you do need to keep in mind is preparing the fruits to make yogurt shake effectively. For smaller fruits, such as berries, you don't need to do anything apart from removing the stem and seed. In the case of pineapples or bananas, cut them up into small, thin pieces before tossing them into the blender. This prevents any chunks forming and floating in the yogurt shake once it is complete.

Recipe

You don't even need to do anything other than toss the ingredients into the blender. Pour the yogurt in first followed by the fruits. The smaller the pieces are, the better they will blend with the yogurt. Press the button and blend them for a good 15 to 20 seconds.

Check once to see whether the yogurt shake is thin and creamy enough. If not, blend for a few more seconds. This is all you have to do to get your yogurt shake ready.

From the time you put out the blender jug and put in the ingredients till the time you drink the yogurt shake, the whole process shouldn't take you more than a minute or so. For the sake of convenience, the average preparation time for yogurt shake is given as 3 minutes. It still isn't too bad for a healthy and tasty beverage you can easily make at home.

So, if you feel like having a fruity shake, forgo milk for once and try yogurt. There is a good chance you will get hooked!

Yogurt Cocktail

Sticking to beverages for the time being, it is the turn of the yogurt cocktail. You can say that this is the 'mature' version of yogurt smoothies, shakes and juices. Making yogurt cocktail is easy and can prove to be a wonderful drink for you to replace breakfast with.

Whether or not you want to add alcohol to it is up to you but some people do add some vodka to it. Anyways, first you need to know how to make yogurt cocktail before you can decide how to have fun with it.

Image Link:
http://www.flickr.com/photos/asimulator/8183196197/

The recipe to make yogurt cocktail is quite similar to that for yogurt juice and smoothies. The main difference is in the ingredients and the way you serve the beverage once it is prepared.

Why Yogurt Cocktail?

You might be wondering why you should try yogurt cocktail when you already have plenty of options as far as yogurt-based beverages are concerned. The main ingredient remains the same but the fact that it is a cocktail adds an extra dimension to it.

For one, yogurt cocktails are incredibly refreshing. This is why I recommend that you have a glass first thing in the morning (without the alcohol of course!). It will have you feeling fresh and alert and drive any semblance of sleep away. You will be ready to take on the world.

Yogurt cocktails are healthy to boot. The ingredients are in your control and completely customizable, much like any other recipe you will go over in this book. This is what makes it convenient for you to make yogurt beverages. You can modify the taste any way you want. Make it tangy or sweet, it will be tasty!

You can serve yogurt cocktails to your guests, putting umbrella straws and lemon on the glass to give it the real cocktail feel.

Supplies & Equipment

The supplies and equipment you require to make yogurt cocktails are limited, as with smoothies and juice. Once again, your blender will have to do the work for you. If you don't have a blender, I recommend you buy one right away so you can try all the recipes in this book.

Since you are making a cocktail, it is better to use tall glasses to serve it. Also, get some fancy straws that add to the cocktail's visual appeal when you serve it. It will help you make a great impression on your visitors.

You will also need a knife and cutting board to slice the lemons and citrus fruits and put them on the glass when serving the cocktail. Apart from this, there is no special equipment or supplies you need to make yogurt cocktail.

Ingredients

It goes without saying that you need yogurt to make yogurt cocktail. How much you use depends on the quantity you want to make. You need ½ cup yogurt to make 1 glass yogurt cocktail so amend the ingredients accordingly.

The rest of the ingredients you have to use depend on the required flavour. For instance, if you want to make tomato yogurt cocktail, you have to use tomato juice, pepper, onion salt and Worcestershire sauce. The sauces are what lend the cocktail zest and zing.

On the other hand, if you are making a sweeter cocktail, let's say strawberry or banana, you can add honey, brown sugar, or any other sweetening agent you feel will lend it the flavour you want.

Recipe

The recipe is quite simple. Just put all the ingredients in a blender and keep blending till they start looking like a cocktail. Don't add the lemon just yet, unless you want its flavour in your yogurt cocktail. The lemon is mainly for adorning the glass in which you serve the drink.

If you turn the settings to 'high' it shouldn't take more than 15 seconds for the ingredients to blend properly and form a smooth and creamy yogurt cocktail. Add ice or chill in the fridge to cool before you drink it. Easy as you like!

Yogurt Smoothie

Smoothies are a wonderful beverage to have for breakfast or late afternoon. Cool, refreshing and nutritious, smoothies pack a fruity punch. No wonder people love drinking smoothies.

Smoothies are usually made with fruits but you can also use certain types of vegetables. Kale, for one, is considered to be one of the best ingredients for a smoothie because of the wide range of health benefits it delivers.

Image Link:
https://picasaweb.google.com/lh/photo/Mk9o2uyN_v7id8n
wrWFW1NMTjNZETYmyPJy0liipFm0?feat=embedwebsite

Smoothies can be made using water, milk or yogurt. Generally, people use milk as it is convenient and the smoothie turns out to be creamy, frothy and quite tasty. Yet, yogurt is an equally viable option.

As you have seen throughout this book, homemade yogurt is considerably healthier than store-bought milk. This is why making smoothies using yogurt is the healthier and more nutritious option.

The major benefit of using yogurt to make smoothies is that it is thicker and creamier than milk. When blended properly, yogurt has a wonderful texture and you will be quite tempted to drink the smoothie right away.

Benefits

There are many benefits of yogurt smoothies, even apart from the health benefits it delivers.

Smoothies Are Tasty

There is little doubt that smoothies are tasty. Based on the ingredients you have used, yogurt smoothies can be incredibly tasty and sweet to drink. Unlike most other 'healthy' drinks, you don't have to force yourself to gulp it down.

Rather, you will have to fight the temptation to drink it several times a day. Given that it doesn't take much time to prepare yogurt smoothies, you can easily make them for breakfast or at any time of the day.

Smoothies Are Fruity

Nutritionists and health experts require that the average person eat at least 3 cups of fruit every day. Even though most fruits are quite tasty, people still don't eat them.

94

Whatever the reason may be, nutrition is one thing you shouldn't ignore. It can have an adverse impact on your health and wellbeing.

So, if you are having a hard time keeping up your fruit consumption at the recommended level, just pop the fruits into the blender along with the yogurt and other ingredients listed below and puree yourself a smoothie.

When you have a smooth, creamy and tasty beverage in front of you, you will find it hard to resist. Take your favourite fruits as the main ingredient. This way, your nutritional needs are fulfilled without you having to eat the fruits raw.

In fact, if you have any fruits lying around the house that you fear will go bad because you are not interested in eating them, use them in a smoothie. It is better than to let them go to waste.

Smoothies Are Customizable

You can choose any fruit you want. There are no restrictions whatsoever. You don't have to choose a particular fruit if you want to enjoy the benefits of yogurt smoothies. This is the great thing about making yogurt smoothies at home.

You have absolute control over the ingredients and you can choose any fruits you want. All you have to do is prepare the ingredients and then put them in the blender along with the yogurt.

I will provide you a few tips to get the fruit ready in the proper way before making smoothies. This way, you can be certain that the smoothie will turn out exactly like you want it to be.

There is no dearth of healthy fruit options. You don't have to select fruits that don't suit your palate. From strawberries to avocadoes, each ingredient you use delivers certain health benefits. So, there are no 'wrong' ingredients when making a yogurt smoothie.

Smoothies Are Filling

By using yogurt as the base for making a smoothie, you also gain the health and nutritional benefits of yogurt. For one, yogurt contains a considerable amount of protein. Your body needs protein on a daily basis. In addition to being a vital nutrient, protein also helps you feel fuller.

As mentioned before, you won't feel hungry after you have eaten a cup of yogurt. What this means is that the smoothies you make are filling as well. You won't have much space left in your tummy once you down a glass of tasty yogurt smoothie.

Instead of drinking it with your breakfast, you can actually replace your breakfast with a smoothie. Nutritionists have verified that yogurt smoothies contain the vital nutrients, vitamins and minerals your body requires to get through the day.

What I would recommend is that you prepare the yogurt smoothie at night and put it in the fridge. In the morning, just take it out, pour it in a glass and drink up. You can call it 'instant breakfast'.

On the other hand, if you are an early riser, you can easily make yogurt smoothie in the morning. Fresh is definitely better.

This is a great option for people who habitually skip breakfast. The main reason they skip the most important meal of the day is that they don't have enough time to prepare breakfast and eat it. In the morning, your body needs energy.

A glass of yogurt smoothie can provide you the boost you need. It will help you get through the day and fulfil all your personal and professional commitments. With a full stomach, you will find yourself more alert and productive. It's all the more reason for you to have yogurt smoothies for breakfast.

Moreover, you can drink a yogurt smoothie any time you don't feel like eating. At times, a person is too tired in the morning to even eat. Rather than skipping meals, which can be harmful to your health, prepare a yogurt smoothie and drink it up.

However, I would not recommend that you go on a yogurt smoothie diet where you don't eat or drink anything else. Nonetheless, it is a great option for you!

Smoothies Contain Fibre

Fruit smoothies contain fibre before you add yogurt into the mix. Fibre is an important nutrient for the body. It boosts the metabolism and helps the digestive system stay in shape.

Fruits generally contain soluble fibre. Soluble fibre not only aids digestion but also helps lower blood cholesterol and sugar levels. So, people suffering from diabetes can drink fruit smoothies without any risk, provided they choose fruits wisely.

Fruits such as apples and pears provide up to 7 grams of fibre per glass of yogurt smoothie. The daily recommended intake is 38 grams for men and 25 grams for women. A couple of yogurt smoothies a day can provide around half of that.

In addition to these benefits, you also have to factor in the benefits of consuming yogurt. This is why I would say that using homemade yogurt, based on the recipes provided in this book, is the ideal option when you are making yogurt smoothies. The active cultures will boost the nutritional value considerably.

Fruit Choices

There are different types of fruits you can use to make yogurt smoothies. It is a good idea for you to be familiar with the classes of fruit you can use and the nutritional value each one provides.

- **Citrus**

  Fruits belonging to the citrus family include grapefruits, oranges and lemons among others. Citrus fruits are the best source of vitamin C. Other nutrients you can get through citrus fruits are folate and potassium.

  Yogurt smoothies made using citrus fruits boost your immune system while also strengthening the cells in your body. Potassium, in particular, is an important nutrient for preserving cardiovascular health. The blood pressure remains in control and the heart's function improves.

- **Berries**

  Berries are among the most popular smoothie ingredients. Grapes, cranberries, blueberries, blackberries, raspberries and strawberries are some of the choices available to you in this category of fruits.

Berries are particularly effective to help your system combat diseases and infections. They are a rich source of antioxidants which prevent cell damage and eliminate toxins and free radicals from the body.

- **Drupes**

  Contrary to popular perception, cherry is not a berry. It belongs to the 'drupe' family along with peaches, plums and apricots. Drupes provide pretty much the same nutrients as citrus fruits.

  Drupes are a great source of beta carotene. Beta carotene is essential for your immune system to function properly. Moreover, it also prevents damage to your eyesight. Drinking yogurt smoothies made with drupes can help keep your vision intact.

- **Melons**

  I don't think I need to detail which fruits belong to the melon family. You have the honey dew melons, casaba, cantaloupes and of course, watermelons. Melons are a rich source of vitamin C, pretty much in the same vein as citrus fruits.

  One specific health benefit of drinking melon-based yogurt smoothies is that the vitamin C you consume will help synthesize the collagen present in your body.

- **Tropical**

  Tropical fruits might just be the best ingredients for a yogurt smoothie. The banana has been a perennial favourite. For some people, a smoothie is incomplete if it doesn't have banana.

Other great tropical fruits you can choose for your smoothies include kiwis, avocadoes, pineapples, mangoes, coconut, papaya and pomegranates.

Tropical fruits are rich in vitamin C, potassium, manganese, and folate. Choosing tropical fruits for your yogurt smoothies benefits your nerves, blood sugar level and also your thyroid gland.

- **Pomes**

   The 'Pomes' family consists mainly of apples and pears. As the saying goes, an apple a day keeps the doctor away. The health benefits of both apples and pears are quite well-known so I won't waste time explaining them.

You probably have a clear idea of the nutrients the fruits you choose to make yogurt smoothies contain. So, pick the ones you feel are the most nutritious and blend a smoothie right away!

Smoothie Tips: Putting the 'Smooth' in Smoothie

Making a smoothie is more than just putting the ingredients in a blender and then pureeing them. You have to achieve the desired thickness and creaminess, otherwise smoothies lose much of their appeal. In this chapter, I will provide you a few tips to follow when making smoothies. In other words, you will learn how to put the 'smooth' in smoothie.

Ice Cubes = Thickness

Probably the easiest technique you can use to make yogurt smoothies thicker is by adding ice cubes to it when you are blending. Even though thickness shouldn't be a concern since you are using yogurt as a base rather than water or milk, sometimes people do end up blending the ingredients too much.

Use Frozen Fruit

Freeze the fruits beforehand in order to improve the yogurt smoothie's thickness. This is a tried and tested technique that works every time. It does mean you have to put the fruit in the freezer well before you intend to make the smoothie.

Not only will the smoothie turn out to be thicker, but considerably cooler than if you were using warm fruit. It may take a few extra seconds of blending but it will be worth the wait.

Liquids First

A common mistake people make when blending smoothies, or even shakes for that matter, is that they put the ingredients in first and then pour the liquids on top. There is a chance the yogurt may get stuck to the ingredients, which makes it difficult to blend them thoroughly. This is the reason you get chunks and pieces of fruit in your smoothies and shakes.

The right way to do this is to put in the liquid ingredients first, including the yogurt, and then tossing in the remaining ingredients. Moreover, it makes the blender's job easier. The liquid at the bottom is easier to blend. This may add a few days, if not months, to the blender's useful life.

Accelerate As You Go

Once you have put all the ingredients in the blender, keeping the tip above in mind, start pureeing at the slowest speed. You have to let the ingredients mix properly and the best way to do this is by accelerating the blade's rotation throughout the process.

Like I said, start at the slowest speed. As you notice the pieces of fruit are breaking up, increase the speed a notch. Take a few seconds and increase the speed again. Keep doing this until you have reached top speed. By now, your yogurt smoothie will be ready and that too in perfect form.

The issue with blenders is that if you puree the ingredients at top speed from the outset, an air bubble forms. You will notice that a vortex emerges when you start blending. The air bubble is inside it and the blades of the blender just keep spinning around the bubble instead of blending the ingredients.

Plus, the blender doesn't shake when you increase the speed gradually.

Follow these tips and you will make the smoothest and creamiest yogurt smoothies you have ever seen. After all, a smoothie is more than just about the taste!

102

Ingredients

There are four ways you can make yogurt smoothies. Each one uses different ingredients but the core items remain the same: fruit and yogurt.

You have to choose a fruit to make the smoothie. The fruit is what lends the yogurt smoothie its flavour, so choose one according to your preferences.

As far as the yogurt is concerned, I would suggest using plain homemade yogurt.

At the same time, you can also use flavoured yogurt to enhance the yogurt smoothie's taste. For instance, add vanilla yogurt to a chocolate smoothie and you will create a wonderful combination.

At the end of the day, it is the recipe that dictates which ingredients you have to use to make the smoothie.

Supplies & Equipment

As you will have guessed by now, there are no particular supplies or equipment you require to prepare yogurt smoothies. The blender will once again come into play and mix the ingredients properly.

Apart from the blender, you will need something to prepare the ingredients in. A mixing bowl will do the trick. Also, you will require a knife to cut, peel and dice the fruits used in the yogurt smoothie.

When serving smoothies, the best option is to use tall glasses. They add to the overall experience of drinking a yogurt smoothie. Keep this in mind particularly when you are serving to guests and visitors.

Recipes

Like I said before, there are four different ways to make yogurt smoothies at home. They depend mainly on the type of fruit you have chosen. I will describe all four in detail to make it easier for you to understand the process.

Berry Smoothie

To make a berry smoothie, you need to have one cup of the berries of your choice. You have the option of selecting one particular berry like strawberry, as well as using more than one type, for instance blueberry and blackberry.

You have to select the berries carefully as not all of them are suitable to use in a smoothie. The ones that are soft or bruised should be discarded. Eat them as they are rather than using them to make yogurt smoothie. Also, look out for berries that have tough skin. The tough skin is hard to blend and will only impede the flavour and texture.

Once you have selected the berries, wash them thoroughly and then remove the stems. You don't want to take in a piece of the stem when you are drinking the yogurt smoothie.

When berries are blended, they tend to assume a gel-like appearance. Mixing them with yogurt alone might not get you the texture you are looking for. A great tip you can use is to add some low-fat milk to the yogurt before you blend the ingredients.

Take ½ cup of milk along with ½ cup of homemade yogurt and pour in the blender. Next, choose a sweetening agent for the smoothie. You can go with honey or brown sugar, to keep it light and healthy. Throw in the berries on top of the yogurt, milk and sweetener.

Puree the ingredients until you are certain there are no chunks or pieces of berry floating in the smoothie. If the results are not to your liking, simply add more yogurt, milk or ice and puree again.

Tropical Smoothie

To make a tropical smoothie, you need to have 1 cup of your favourite tropical fruit. As with the berries, you can choose one particular fruit or make a combo, such as mixing pineapple and kiwi or mango and guava. Tropical smoothies have a Pina colada like feel, making them more appealing.

Clean the fruits thoroughly and then cut them into small pieces. For the sake of convenience, ½ inch chunks are ideal for a smoothie. The size ensures they are processed easily by the blender and you don't find them floating in your beverage when you are drinking it.

The choice of yogurt for a tropical smoothie is exciting. Plain yogurt will serve your purpose but it is better to go with something that is a little tangier. Tropical fruits are incredibly juicy and you need yogurt that counterbalances that quality to a certain extent.

In my opinion, Greek yogurt is your best option for a tropical smoothie. It is tangy, thick and complements the taste and texture of tropical fruits when they are blended.

As far as the sweetening is concerned, you won't actually need to put much effort there. Most tropical fruits are quite sweet. In case you feel they aren't sweet enough, you can simply cut up a banana and toss it into the blender with the other ingredients. Banana is a tropical fruit and it helps maintain a consistent tropical feel for the smoothie.

Still, if you want to sweeten the yogurt smoothie up a little, I would recommend using fresh fruit juice. ¼ cup pineapple or mango juice ought to do the job. You can also use orange juice and lend a touch of citrus to your tropical yogurt smoothie.

So, the ingredients will consist of 1 cup of tropical fruit, ¼ cup of fruit juice and ¾ cup of yogurt. Blend the ingredients until they are mixed smoothly and appear like the perfect yogurt smoothie. In case you want to increase the smoothie's thickness, add some yogurt and blend again. If you want to reduce the thickness, add more juice.

Autumn Smoothie

Pomes are considered to be autumn fruits. You can make an autumn smoothie by using apple or pear, or both, as the main ingredient. When preparing an apple or pear to make a yogurt smoothie, you not only have to cut it into small pieces, but also peel it. The fruit's skin does not blend properly and makes the yogurt smoothie less appetizing.

So, start off by washing the fruit/s and peeling them. Remove the stems and seeds as they too can reduce the appeal of the yogurt smoothie. Next, cut the fruit up into small pieces, ½ inch chunks being the ideal size.

In the autumn smoothie, you have to use thick yogurt. My suggestion is that you make plain yogurt and then use the tips I provided in the chapter on plain yogurt to increase its thickness. You will need 1 cup of the thickest yogurt you can find.

For the autumn smoothie, you can add a couple of spices that are commonly associated with the fall season. Cinnamon is a great option but you can also use nutmeg if you want. Since they both lend a tremendous flavour to the yogurt smoothie, you can add ½ teaspoon of each.

For sweetening, maple syrup is the best choice for autumn smoothies. Put 1 tablespoon of maple syrup over the yogurt and add the spices when starting to make the yogurt smoothie.

Add the fruits to the ingredients and turn the blender on. Keep blending till the mixture becomes frothy and creamy. You can sprinkle some cinnamon on top of the smoothie for garnishing when serving it. It will also enhance the taste of the beverage.

Tropical Berry Smoothie

The fourth type of smoothie you can make is by combining tropical fruits with berries. This combination is quite popular and strawberry & banana is one of the most popular fruit smoothie flavours in the world.

I have detailed the process to prepare berries and tropical fruits when whipping up a yogurt smoothie, so you don't need to know anything else about it. In all, you need to have one cup of fruit, and make sure the fruits are adequately balanced when you are filling up the cup.

Tropical fruits are juicier and in some instances, sweeter than berries. If you are using banana, I would suggest adding only 1 banana to the recipe. The rest of the fruit should be made up by berries. This is done so that the banana's sweetness is offset by the berries and a strong flavour emerges from the combination.

I don't think you will need to add sweeteners to a tropical berry smoothie. The fruits are sweet enough already so you don't have to pour a spoonful of stevia on top. Still, you can add a sweetening agent should you feel the need to. There is nothing stopping you from using it!

For the tropical berry smoothie, vanilla yogurt is the best option. Vanilla's taste blends perfectly with fruits and creates a wonderful flavour. You can also go for any other fruit-flavoured yogurt if you want. It will only add to the sweetness and taste of the smoothie you make. Plain yogurt is also an option.

You know the drill. Pour the yogurt into the blender followed by the remaining ingredients. Blend till the mixture takes on the appearance of a yogurt smoothie.

So, now you know the four different ways you can make a smoothie. It all depends on the fruit, or the combination of fruits you are using to make the smoothie.

There are no restrictions but I would suggest you don't go for any unconventional combinations. Pomegranate and kiwis are tasty fruits but I bet no one can tell you what they taste like when combined. It is better to leave that to your imagination.

You might wonder why I haven't outlined a recipe for yogurt smoothies made using prunes, melons and citrus fruits. I didn't forget. It is just that I don't need to describe the recipes separately.

This is because the recipe for tropical fruits works for citrus fruits. Melon yogurt smoothies can be made following the autumn smoothie recipe. As far as the prunes are concerned, you can use them in any recipe but make sure you remove the skin.

Even though there are different recipes to make yogurt smoothies at home, all of them are simple and easy to follow. Plus it won't take you more than a few minutes to get the ingredients ready. Blending them for a minute or so will get you the perfect yogurt smoothie.

In addition to following the recipes closely, you would also do well to keep the tips regarding smoothie thickness in mind. Stick to the instructions and you won't regret spending your time and energy making yogurt smoothies.

An Important Tip

The recipes to make yogurt smoothies are straightforward and easy to follow. However, they are tricky when it comes to making multiple servings. The thing with making yogurt smoothies is that the ingredients are quite dense and take up a lot of space in the blender.

Now, doubling the ingredients should enable you to make two glasses of yogurt smoothie at once. But, this cannot be done if there isn't room enough in the blender. You will get the ingredients in easily but after blending, the mixture will rise and might spill over the sides.

Even though it means more work for you, I will recommend that you make each smoothie serving separately. There is no harm in trying to make multiple servings at once. If your blender is big enough, you might be able to pull this off and save time and effort.

One other thing you should keep in mind is about storing yogurt smoothies in the fridge. Most people prefer to freeze their smoothies at night and then take them on the go when they leave for work. This way, they don't have to spend any time for breakfast.

The issue here is that yogurt smoothies tend to expand once they are put in the freezer. So, if the container is filled to the brim with yogurt smoothie, there is every chance that the smoothie will expand and the container will not have enough space for it.

Use a large container or bottle, leaving some room for the yogurt smoothie to expand when it starts freezing.

Making yogurt smoothies at home is no rocket science. Neither do you have to be a cooking expert to get the right flavour and thickness. Use this chapter as a guide to make perfect smoothies that you will just love drinking again and again. Bottoms up!

Yogurt Cake

That's right! You love yogurt, and there is no reason why you can't have it in something as irresistible as cake. In this chapter, we learn all about yogurt cake, and we will end by teaching you a recipe to make one at home.

You will notice that this recipe is vastly different to the other ones I have included in this book. Making yogurt cake requires you to bring your baking skills to the fore. As far as the other recipes are concerned, you simply have to combine the ingredients properly.

Image Link:
http://www.flickr.com/photos/irisphotos/5422227637/

What is Yogurt Cake?

Yogurt cake is like another cake, except here, yogurt is the distinguishing factor. It should also be remembered that while yogurt is a delicious addition to any dairy item imaginable, it also serves as a great substitute to many high-fat baking ingredients, like shortening, oil, butter, and sour cream, to name a few. It also adds to the cake's aesthetic appeal. Of course, this doesn't matter much in the culinary world. But hey, everyone loves creamy texture and softness in their cakes, right?

Why Eat Yogurt Cakes?

Well, because they taste good! This is why most of us eat what we eat. However, if you allow me to go into the nitty-gritty of nutrition and baking, eating yogurt cake provides you with a host of health benefits.

You are already familiar with the benefits of all types of yogurt, but let's go over some cool reasons to eat cake:

> A slice of cake gives us much needed energy during the day because of the flour and sugar present in it

> Milk and eggs give us necessary protein that makes our teeth and bones healthy

> Fruit cakes have all the health benefits of the fruits present in them

> The butter and icing give us oils and fats, but these are also needed for the regular functioning of the human body

> Many cakes have chocolate. Dark chocolate especially, has been scientifically proven to reduce cholesterol and lower blood pressure

> Cakes add 'flavour' to every occasion on and off the calendar!

112

Of course, we are not suggesting that you go cake crazy. Everything should be consumed in moderation, so the saying goes. But coming back to our chapter title, the point I am trying to make it that by baking and eating yogurt cake, you are actually bringing the individual benefits of these two items together!

General Baking Tips Using Yogurt

Before moving on to the recipe of baking a yogurt cake, let us first go over some general tips on how yogurt can be incorporated as a healthy ingredient in your favourite baked products. Remember, these instructions are to be followed if you want to strictly lower some calories. Otherwise, you are free to use all the butter and oil you like!

When Using Butter

If you are baking something and the recipe calls for butter, here's what you need to do. Replace half butter with around an equal quantity of yogurt, such as ½ cup yogurt for ½ cup butter.

When Using Oils

If some recipe mentions oils on the list of ingredients, you can always replace half the oil with ¾ of the amount of yogurt. As an example, half of 1 cup of oil will be replaced by a ½ cup of yogurt (and perhaps a couple of extra tablespoons).

When Using Sour Cream

Want to make a sour cream baking recipe healthier with yogurt? Replace the entire quantity listed in the recipe with yogurt.

When Using Water and Milk

Ok, these items are not something that will make you phobic about weight issues. I am just saying that even liquids like water and milk can be replaced by yogurt. For instance, you can substitute ¼ of either liquid. This of course is not a health benefit, but using yogurt will help you achieve a creamy texture. Not to mention, the taste will also be enhanced!

As it turns out, yogurt has other uses than just being used in smoothies! So let's go over all the things we need to bake a yogurt cake.

Supplies & Equipment

Making a yogurt cake doesn't require any special equipment. Here we are focusing on the strawberry yogurt cake or the *gâteau au yaourt* as the French call it. Nevertheless, for the sake of clarity, let us have a quick rundown of the things we will need to make this French delicacy materialize.

You can manage this one without a mixer, and you won't need a whole collection of bowls to whisk a plethora of ingredients. Get a 9-inch spring form cake pan (preparation tips below). Of course you will need an oven that can heat up to 350^0. Keep some foil at hand to cover the base you create.

Ingredients

To start off, you will need 1-1½ cups of yogurt. Purely for the taste, I prefer that you go with your homemade plain yogurt. Since you have the luxury of experimenting with the cake's taste, you can opt for flavoured yogurt as well. This will lend a fruity flavour to the cake, making it tastier!

Next, you need a wee bit of nutmeg, but it should be freshly ground.

You will also require 2 ½ cups of vanilla and 2/3 cup olive oil. You will also need flour, since you have to bake the cake. I suggest using almond flour as it is not just tasty, but incredibly healthy as well. However, it is up to you to choose any type of flour you want. The flour has to be 2 ½ cups as well.

In addition to the flour, you will also require ¾ teaspoon baking soda, 2 ½ teaspoons of baking powder and ½ teaspoon of salt. 3 eggs are a must and you need to get 1 ¼ cups of brown sugar.

Recipe

- Firstly, you have to heat the oven to 350⁰F. Part of the preparation also involves using baking spray on the cake pan. You also need to the line the bottom with parchment.
- Take the yogurt, olive oil, sugar, eggs, and vanilla in a container. Whisk them together
- To this concoction, add the nutmeg, salt, soda, flour, and baking powder
- Stir vigorously until no lumps remain
- Pour this mixture into the spring form pan
- Bake for up to an hour (maximum)
- Towards the end of the baking duration, cover the pan with foil if you see the top browning
- Place the cake on a cooling rack. Leave it there for 10 minutes
- Remove from the pan and serve warm or at room temperature

Note that this recipe makes 8-10 servings. To keep the cake for several days, make sure you wrap it well.
Simply increase the ingredients if you want to make more servings.

Yogurt Ice Cream

People often wonder what the difference is between frozen yogurt and yogurt ice cream. We have covered frozen yogurt in detail in one of the earlier chapters of this book. You can modify the flavour and texture of the yogurt but at its core, it remains frozen.

As far as yogurt ice cream is concerned, it probably came about as a happy accident. The basic premise of yogurt ice cream is that it is a mix between frozen yogurt and homemade ice cream. People who have made ice cream at home before will not have any problem following this recipe and making it to perfection.

Image Link:
http://www.flickr.com/photos/stuart_spivack/2871241000/

Now, you don't necessarily have to follow the recipe for making ice cream to make yogurt ice cream. The recipe for yogurt ice cream is quite different but it's not difficult to follow. You simply have to go over it step by step and you won't face any trouble making yogurt ice cream at home.

Benefits of Yogurt Ice Cream

Making yogurt ice cream at home enables you to enjoy the benefits of yogurt as well as that of eating ice cream. You might wonder if there are any real health benefits of eating ice cream. After all, it is a dairy product that contains sugar. Healthy is not the word one would usually use to describe it. But, surprisingly it provides a host of health benefits to you.

Low Glycemic Index

For one, ice cream has a low glycemic index. This means it helps keep your blood sugar level stable and prevents constant fluctuations.

The benefit can be compounded by using Greek yogurt to make yogurt ice cream. Greek yogurt is whey-free and thus does not contain too many calories. Hence, the risk of your blood sugar level rising is minimal.

Full of Calcium

Ice cream is full of calcium. Your bones need calcium, a lot of it to stay strong and fight off illnesses like arthritis. Homemade yogurt also has high calcium content and it will increase your calcium consumption per serving.

This means you can make up most of your daily required calcium intake by eating a cup of yogurt ice cream every day. A single cup of yogurt ice cream will provide over 20% of the calcium you need to eat in one day.

Loaded with Proteins
Yogurt ice cream is one of the most protein-rich dairy foods you will come across. Both calcium and protein are essential nutrients. The great thing is that you can ensure you don't suffer a deficiency of either of the two by eating a cup or two of yogurt ice cream daily.

It's Not Fattening
You might be surprised to read that yogurt ice cream is not fattening. Now, I am assuming that you are going to use homemade yogurt to make the ice cream, based on one of the recipes I have provided in this book. Thus, the yogurt contains no fat at all.

Even commercial ice cream is not fattening. According to the nutritional table, ice cream contains 15% of the daily fat requirement for a person. That is a small percentage and is used when your body requires energy. So, if anyone tells you that eating ice cream can make you fat, you know better than to believe them, unless of course you binge on ice cream on a daily basis.

The health benefits of yogurt ice cream might not be easily understood as the perception we have of ice cream is that it is unhealthy.

The 'Cold' Myth
There is a common misconception regarding yogurt ice cream. It states that eating it can cause cold and flu. The reason for this is easy to understand, as ice cream is definitely cold and cold foods and beverages are considered to be the cause of throat related ailments.

The thing with yogurt ice cream is that it starts melting rapidly once you put it in your mouth. The temperature of your body ensures the ice cream does not stay solid for too long. Once it starts melting, its temperature increases considerably.

The bottom-line is that by the time yogurt ice cream enters the oesophageal passage, it's not as cold as when you started eating it. Cold beverages are likely to cause a cold and flu as they retain the same temperature even when they have passed through the mouth.

Supplies & Equipment

As far as the equipment is concerned, you can use an ice cream maker if you have one. The recipe for frozen yogurt also suggests the use of an ice cream maker. However, if you don't own an ice cream maker, you don't have to buy one. You can easily make yogurt ice cream without it.

The supplies & equipment you need to make yogurt ice cream at home include:

- 1 saucepan
- 1 small mixing bowl
- 1 egg beater/whisk
- 1 heatproof bowl
- 1 large bowl
- 1 fork
- 1 storage container
- 1 metal sieve

You will understand the purpose for each of these utensils and instruments when we go over the recipe for yogurt ice cream.

Ingredients

The usual suspects to make ice cream all come into the picture when you set out to make yogurt ice cream. From milk to sugar to salt, the ingredients are quite similar. This is why I said that if you have made ice cream at home before, you won't find it too hard to make yogurt ice cream.

- **1 cup milk:** Use low-fat milk to make the yogurt ice cream healthy and nutritious. You can also use whole milk.
- **12 ounces yogurt:** The choice of yogurt is yours. I would recommend using Greek yogurt because it is whey-free. However, feel free to use homemade plain yogurt. You can also use flavoured yogurt, but make sure it is consistent with the flavour of the ice cream you are making.
- **¾ cup sugar:** A little indulgence never hurt anybody so you can use sugar when making yogurt ice cream. However, if you want to keep the recipe sugar-free, you can use brown sugar. Any other sweetening agents might not produce the desired results.
- **2 egg yolks:** Put the egg yolks into a small bowl and start whisking. Beat them properly before you start making yogurt ice cream. The recipe requires you to use beaten egg yolks.
- **¾ cup cream:** The choice of cream is again up to you but I would suggest you keep it consistent with the type of milk you are using. For instance, if you are using low-fat milk, use low-fat cream as well.

These are the key ingredients that go into making yogurt ice cream at home. Have them ready and prepared when you start using this recipe. This will reduce the time it takes for you to make yogurt ice cream.

For the mixture you will use to make yogurt ice cream, you will need the following ingredients:

- 1 cup of the fresh fruit/ flavour you want to use
- ¼ teaspoon vanilla extract
- A pinch of salt
- ½ cup sugar
- 2 cups cream

These ingredients will help you create the perfect ice cream mixture, which you can combine with yogurt to form a delicious serving of yogurt ice cream.

Recipe

Now, here you have to bring your culinary skills to the fore. Most of the recipes I have covered so far involve you cutting and slicing ingredients and putting them in a blender with yogurt and milk. This is not the case when making yogurt ice cream.

You have to be more careful and each step has to be completed precisely or else the final product will not be worth the effort you put into it.

There are two parts to this recipe. The first part involves preparing the base for the ice cream, which is primarily yogurt. The second part involves getting the custard mixture ready that will be used to flavour the yogurt ice cream.

Part 1:

➢ Take the saucepan and put the milk, cream and sugar into it. You don't have to mix them just yet. Turn the stove on to medium heat and cook until

122

bubbles start appearing. Once again, you have to prevent the milk from boiling, so be careful.

Start stirring the mixture when it begins to heat up. On medium heat, this would mean around 4 to 5 minutes after you put the saucepan on the stove. This is around the time it would take for the milk to start heating up.

- ➢ Use a plastic cup to retrieve ½ cup of the mixture that you have heated on the stove. Be cautious when you are taking the mixture, as it will be extremely hot at the time.
- ➢ Put the beaten egg yolks into a small mixing bowl and pour the ½ cup mixture you have extracted. Whisk egg yolks and the mixture together till they blend well and combine.
- ➢ Bring the heat down to low and pour the contents of the small mixing bowl back into the saucepan. Once again, be very careful when doing this as any spillage could cause a burn.
- ➢ Let the mixture cook for around 5 minutes on low heat. By this time, the mixture will have thickened enough that it should coat any spoon or fork you put into it.
- ➢ Now, take the heatproof bowl and put a metal sieve over it. Through the sieve pour the mixture into the heatproof bowl.
- ➢ Fill a large bowl with water and put some ice in it. Place the heatproof bowl into the large bowl till it cools down. You can also put the bowl in the fridge if you feel that is easier for you to do. Either way, it will take a few hours for the mixture to cool down sufficiently.

➤ Once it is cool enough to handle, take a fork and start beating the mixture. Make sure the yogurt is completely smooth before you stop beating it.

Part 2:

To make it easier to understand, I am going to follow the recipe for strawberry yogurt ice cream.

➤ Take a cup of fresh strawberries. Remove the stems and seeds, also ensuring that the strawberries are clean. Cut into small pieces.

➤ Put the cream, sugar, vanilla extract, strawberries and salt into the blender.

➤ Blend the mixture for a minute or so. Keep going till the strawberry chunks have been completely blended and the ingredients are mixed properly. The mixture should be thick and frothy.

Once you have completed both parts of the recipe, you have to combine the two. The custard mixture will be poured into the yogurt and mixed properly.

To freeze the ice cream, you can follow any of the methods which were described in the chapter on frozen yogurt. In case you have an ice cream maker, follow the instructions provided to learn how to freeze ice cream in it.

The Flavour

The most important part of making yogurt ice cream is choosing a flavour for it. If you want to make fruity ice cream, you can use fresh fruits, but it is also possible that you may prefer a non-fruit flavour such as chocolate.

The great thing is that you don't have to limit yourself to a certain flavour or a specific type of ingredient. Most people have a favourite ice cream flavour and they stick with it if they want.

At the same time, I would recommend that you don't use artificial flavouring. Though it does deliver the taste you are looking for, it is not healthy. Fresh ingredients are far tastier and their flavour is more pronounced. In other words, they are a better choice for yogurt ice cream.

That being said, I still would like to make it clear that you can choose any flavour you want. The preference for ice cream flavour varies from person to person. Who am I to ask you to select one flavour over another?

As you can see, making yogurt ice cream is not too hard. If you are confused about choosing between frozen yogurt and yogurt ice cream, I would say you try both and then determine which one is better for you. They are equally nutritious and healthy, so it is a win-win situation.

Yogurt Salad

Salads are synonymous with healthy eating and weight loss. However, many people are seen using salad dressings made from cream and mayo. So much for healthy eating!

Commercially available products are full of fats and other preservatives, the effects of which on your body are better left to the imagination. Yet, people love the taste of sour cream, mayo and garlic sauce. They cannot seem to get enough.

If you really want to enjoy the taste and benefits of salads, why not add yogurt to them? This section is all about yogurt-based salads and how you can use them to enhance your meals without comprising the calories.

The strange thing is that yogurt salads aren't widely consumed. Given the popularity of salads in general, one would assume that people at least know of salads that use yogurt as an ingredient. The lack of awareness is startling to say the least.

Health Benefits of Eating Salads

Although salads are made with few ingredients, they are one of the best meals out there if you go strictly by nutritional value. A salad is a complete meal even though most people eat them as appetizers.

Just salad greens serve as a great source of calcium, iron, potassium and vitamin B. Other ingredients, like tomatoes, and sweet peppers provide essential antioxidants.

Not to mention the high fibre and low calories you get by eating salad on a regular basis. And you cannot ignore the many health benefits of eating yogurt, as I have been stressing throughout this book. Yogurt salad is easy to make and great for your health. All you have to do is get the ingredients ready and then yogurt-ize them!

Smoked Salmon Salad

Smoked salmon salad is one of the most popular salads you will find. It is made using sour cream, which you can replace with any of the yogurt you made at home. The stress is on how you can replace sour cream in this delicious salad with yogurt.

Use ½ cup Greek yogurt and mix it with garlic and lemon juice, sprinkling some salt and pepper for seasoning. Once the salmon is ready, pour the yogurt dressing over it before serving.

Yogurt Salad Dressing for Chicken & Tangerine

Honey ginger yogurt salad dressing goes together fabulously with a bowl of chicken and tangerine. For one thing, it is 100% fat-free, unless you are using full-fat yogurt.

The ingredients used are as follows:

➢ You need 1/8 cup plain Greek yogurt (low fat or non-fat, your call).

➢ You also need grated ginger root (anywhere from ½-1 tablespoon, depending on how much you want) and rice vinegar (1 tablespoon).

➢ You also require granulated garlic (1/4 teaspoon) and honey (1 teaspoon).

To prepare the dressing, simply mix all these ingredients together. Of course, in the presence of ginger, this may not be the "smoothest" of all salad dressing, but then, everyone likes chunky dressing once in a while.

Yogurt-Based Herb Salad Dressing

This has "healthy" written all over it. Start by putting finely chopped fresh summer herbs in a small bowl. You can use anything in the range of spring onions, garlic greens, onion weed etc.

Add salt and pepper, along with some lemon zest, as you mix them around. Add plain yogurt, and continue mixing. Add some herb flowers for presentation. Simple as that!

Yogurt Tahini Salad Dressing for Meatballs

To prepare the salad, you need mixed salad greens, tomatoes, olive oil, and salt. Now you have to make the yogurt sauce.

Get Greek yogurt (200g), tahini (1 tablespoon), lime juice (2 tablespoons), roasted garlic, and salt. Mix these together, and add a little water if the dressing is too thick.

Once the meatballs are prepared, serve them with tomatoes, salad greens, and olive oil, and pour the yogurt dressing on top.

Yogurt Salad Dressing and Roasted Cauliflower

Roasted cauliflower is a great addition to items like cooked brown rice. However, you can further enhance the taste by preparing yogurt based salad dressing to go with roasted cauliflower.

Get the ingredients together:
- Drained chick peas (1 cup)
- Chopped green onions (1/2 cup)
- Yogurt

Place yogurt in a small bowl and slowly add olive oil while stirring. Once the mixture is smooth, add the other ingredients and allow it to sit at temperature for about 20 minutes. Drizzle over the rice and cauliflower when ready.

Organic Plain Yogurt Dressing

This is another herb-rich salad dressing, but this time you have to use plain yogurt. The ingredients are:

- 4 tablespoons plain yogurt
- 1 cup sun gold
- 2 tablespoons maple syrup
- 2 cups herb leaves (of your choice)
- 1 cup ripe strawberries (quartered)
- 2 cups radishes (sliced)

To prepare the salad, take a medium bowl and place all the ingredients in it except yogurt and maple syrup. You have to mix the yogurt and maple syrup in a separate bowl and then pour it over the salad.

Plain Yogurt Dressing to go with Arugula

This recipe is for 2 servings. Take 1 tablespoon of plain yogurt and mix it together with ½ tablespoon lime juice. Toss the arugula in with the dressing and you can even add 2 tablespoons of granola on top.

Asparagus with Yogurt

Here what you'll need:

- 7 ounces Greek yogurt
- Asparagus
- 2 lemons
- 1 tablespoon chopped parsley
- Salt & pepper, to taste
- 2 hardboiled eggs

After chopping off its hard ends, cook the asparagus any way you like. Slice one lemon and set aside. Do the same with the eggs.

Take a bowl, and mix in the Greek yogurt along with the lemon juice. Add 1 tablespoon of parsley as you continue to mix.

On the cooked asparagus, sprinkle salt, pepper, and lemon. Pour the yogurt dressing on top and serve.

Yogurt Dressing with Coleslaw

➤ Take a large bowl and mix together chopped vegetables like cabbage (both red and green), broccoli, carrot, and scallions.
➤ Take a medium bowl and mix together Greek yogurt, vinegar, mayonnaise, lemon juice, and garlic.
➤ Cover the two bowls and leave them to them chill.
➤ Before serving, thinly slice an apple after removing its core, and add to the vegetable mixture.
➤ Finally, mix together the contents of both bowls.

Persian Yogurt Salad

Here is the list of ingredients:

- 38 ounces plain yogurt
- 2 tablespoons dried dill weed
- 2 minced garlic cloves
- 1 chopped cucumber
- Salt and pepper to taste

To make the salad, blend together the yogurt, dill weed, garlic, salt, and pepper in a medium bowl. Then put in the cucumber slices and mix. Cover the bowl and refrigerate overnight.

Prepare any of the salads or dressings and you have a wonderful side dish for dinner or lunch. If you don't feel too hungry, you can have it as a meal. The nutrients will ensure you feel full after having the salad.

It does appear like a radical idea, adding yogurt to salads. But the nutritional value and flavour of homemade yogurt makes it a great option. You simply have to process the ingredients and pour the yogurt over the salad.

The recipes listed in this chapter are just the tip of the iceberg. You can add yogurt to practically any salad that uses dressing.

Yogurt Sundae

Do you love sundaes? Well, who doesn't? But it is unlikely that you have ever tried a yogurt sundae before. Sundaes are not only a sweet treat, but can also be eaten for breakfast if they're healthy. Much like smoothies, sundaes contain the nutrients you need to keep going throughout the day.

Unless you have encountered a 'Make Your Own Sundae' bar at any event, I would assume that you buy your sundaes from the market. Now, there is nothing wrong with that, but you can just as easily make them at home. Adding yogurt to the recipe will make them tastier and healthier.

As mentioned above, you can eat the sundae for breakfast. Yet, there are no limitations whatsoever. Whenever you feel like having a sweet, refreshing snack, make yourself a yogurt sundae and tuck in. The entire exercise won't take you more than half an hour.

The Sundae vs. Parfait Debate

You might be thinking that parfaits and sundaes are one and the same thing. It is true that most of the ingredients used to make them are similar. In fact, they are quite alike in appearance as well. So, when you know how to make yogurt parfait and the recipe is incredibly easy, why should you take any interest in learning how to make yogurt sundaes?

The main difference is in the approach towards making the item. Sundaes require you to display your culinary skills and prove that you are adept at managing things in the kitchen. On the other hand, parfaits are more or less an amalgamation of ingredients that you put together.

Hence, it can be said that sundaes are more difficult than parfaits, but they taste wonderful and you will enjoy the experience of making them. This doesn't at all mean that you have to be an expert chef to make a yogurt sundae. It is comparatively difficult than making yogurt parfait, but on the whole, it is a simple and straightforward recipe.

If you follow the steps properly, you shouldn't have any trouble making perfect sundaes that you will absolutely love eating.

Supplies & Equipment

You can give your blender some time off as you don't need to use it to make yogurt sundaes. As you will have seen in most recipes, the blender plays an important part, but not this time.

In fact, it doesn't take much for you to make yogurt sundaes at home. You require a mixing bowl, the larger the better. Also, you will need something to whisk the ingredients with.

Unlike parfaits, yogurt sundaes cannot be served in a glass. You have to use proper serving dishes for them. My choice has been transparent glass serving dishes because you can see the ingredients as you are eating the sundae. This way, you can control the distribution of flavour.

Ingredients

Like I said earlier, the ingredients used to make yogurt sundaes are pretty similar to the ones used to make yogurt parfaits. One of my favourite yogurt sundae flavours is a berry tropical citrus concoction that is incredibly tasty.

The ingredients you need to make 2 servings of yogurt sundae are:

- 1 cup plain yogurt – You can use plain or Greek yogurt if you don't want the yogurt's flavour overriding the ingredients you add to the sundae later on. On the other hand, you can choose to use flavoured yogurt to enhance the sundae's taste.
- 2 tablespoons raw honey – Raw honey is a great sweetening agent and is healthier than granulated and processed sugar. This way, you can keep your sundae healthy and nutritious.
- ¼ teaspoon vanilla extract – The vanilla extract is a must for all sweet treats you make using yogurt as the base. However, if you are using vanilla yogurt in the recipe, then you don't have to add vanilla extract.
- ½ cup fresh orange juice – In my favourite yogurt sundae recipe, fresh orange juice is what puts the citrus in the sundae. The nutrients and minerals contained within fresh orange juice further enhance the health benefits of eating yogurt sundae.
- ¾ cup berries – You have a free hand as far as berries are concerned. My picks have to be strawberry, blueberry and blackberry. You can use only one type of berry, but the more the merrier. Make sure the berries you use combine to make ¾ cup.
- ½ cup tropical fruits – You again have the license to choose whichever tropical fruits you want to use in the recipe. The quantity has to be ½ cup. I usually go for mangoes and kiwis though I have used bananas on occasion.
- ½ cup granola or cereal – The granola or cereal is to make the sundae crunchy and crispy. If there is one

ingredient that you can skip when making yogurt sundae, it is perhaps this one. In case you don't like eating granola or cereal (hard to believe), you don't have to add either of them.

Recipe

You have to put in a little more effort to make yogurt sundae than you had to for yogurt parfait. But it's not mission impossible. Since the recipe is simple, you won't have much trouble following it.

➢ Prepare the fruits to use in the recipe. Make sure the berries are stem-free. Also remove the seeds from the berries. This will make them more palatable and even enhance their taste.

➢ For tropical fruits, cut them into small chunks. Smaller is better as you aren't going to process it in a blender. This will make it easier for you to mix the fruits with other ingredients.

➢ Squeeze orange juice just before you start making the sundae. Since it hardly takes a couple of minutes, I don't think it would be too big of a hassle. This will ensure the juice is fresh and loaded with nutrients.

➢ Take a medium-sized bowl and put in all the fruit that you are using in the sundae. Make sure you select a bowl that is large enough for the 1 ¼ cup of fruit (berries and tropical fruits combined). Pour orange juice in the bowl and stir gently. Keep stirring till the fruits mix properly with the orange juice.

➢ Using another small bowl, combine the rest of the ingredients except for the granola/cereal. You have

135

to mix, whisk or stir yogurt, raw honey and vanilla extract together. You have to make sure they mix together properly and become one. This mixture will form the base of your yogurt sundae so mix thoroughly.

➤ Now comes the tricky part. This is where you have to be careful with the ingredients or else the whole recipe could crumble. Put the 2 serving dishes out. First, you have to pour ¼ of the yogurt mixture into each dish. Then, add ¼ of the fruit and orange juice mixture. Next, put ¼ of the granola/cereal you have selected for the recipe.

➤ Once the first layer is complete, repeat the process. The granola/cereal comes at the end and will be at the top of the yogurt sundae.

The yogurt sundae is ready to eat. As you are making yogurt sundae in the serving dishes, you don't have to transfer it to any other dish for serving. You can eat the sundae right away.

If you want to eat the sundae chilled, cover the dishes with lids and put them in the fridge. It won't take more than a couple of hours for the sundae to get nice and cool.

One trick you can use to make a chilled yogurt sundae is by freezing the fruits in advance. You will recall that this is a technique you follow when making yogurt ice cream. There is no patent stopping you from trying it when making a yogurt sundae.

So, as you can see, making a yogurt sundae is not as difficult as it may seem. The preparation of the ingredients for the sundae is hardly any work. Yet, you have to be careful when pouring the layers into serving dishes. If you pour too much or too little, the balance of the yogurt sundae is disturbed. The key is to get even layers or else you might not enjoy eating it.

Yogurt sundaes are a great replacement for breakfast. You can also have one as a late afternoon snack or as dessert after dinner.

Hence, yogurt sundae can be eaten at any time of the day with (or in lieu) of any meal. Just make sure you get the ingredients right and then pour it out with precision. The yogurt sundae will turn out to be perfect when you follow the recipe step by step.

Conclusion

With this, we have come to the end of the book. It has been a long journey. At times, I felt as though I wouldn't be able to complete what I had set out to achieve, but thankfully I did. I have reached my goal and the feeling it brings is great.

My aim with this book was to enlighten you about the many recipes you can follow using yogurt as the main ingredient. In my opinion, yogurt is among the most underrated and underused dairy products.

After reading this book, you will see that yogurt can be a part of every meal you have. From breakfast to dinner to even the side dishes you have with the main course, yogurt can be a major part of your daily diet.

It is not just its taste that compelled me to write this book, but the numerous health benefits it delivers. I think it is safe to say that keeping the nutritional properties of yogurt in mind, one can easily say that it is one of the healthiest food items you can eat. Plus, it is easy to make.

Throughout the book, I have tried to be consistent with the tone and have tried to cover the recipes in as much detail as possible.

Once again, I would like to thank every person who helped me write this book in whichever way, especially my family for the patience they showed.

I hope you enjoyed reading the book from cover to cover and have even more fun making yogurt at home and trying out the recipes. It's all about trying. All I would say is that there is no harm in trying.

So, if you are looking to improve your health and nutrition, adding yogurt to your daily diet is the way to go. Use this book as a guide to make your own yogurt and enjoy it in all its natural goodness.

Here's to tasty, healthy yogurt! Cheers!

About the Author

Ian Owers is a food connoisseur from North East England. His travels across the world have allowed him to taste some of the most delectable and scrumptious cuisines, but his real passion is homemade recipes, hence, this detailed book on making dairy products at home.

He believes in the do-it-yourself and healthy approach, which is why Ian prefers to consume food that can be made at home easily instead of buying. This book is his first homemade recipe book and he plans to release more recipe books in the future to help people live healthier and more content lives.

While his true passion lies in various types of yogurt such as frozen, Greek etc, he has an affinity towards other dairy products. The simple recipes allow just about anyone to make a wide array of delicious yet healthy dairy products.

CPSIA information can be obtained at www.ICGtesting.com
Printed in the USA
BVOW11s1817081215

429720BV00008BA/137/P